Shewbird Mountain

The Devil's Post Office
In the Shewbird Mountain

The Devil's Post Office is a *cave* hidden deep in the Shewbird Mountain. This cave was a 'forbidden' place when I was a child growing up in the Matheson Cove, in Clay County, North Carolina. My sisters and I were never allowed to hike up to the Shewbird Mountain and explore the Devil's Post Office. However, in earlier times this cave was an exciting place for teenagers to visit. Even older folks who believed in the legends of the Shewbird Mountain would make the climb to the Devil's Post Office. It seemed there was once an old Cherokee Indian named Shewbird, living near the foot of the mountain. That is the reason that folks call the mountain "Shewbird."

While doing some research, I was told by some very honest folks that they did indeed write letters to the Devil and took them to the Devil's Post Office. They generally chose Sunday afternoons to hike the mountain and take their letters to the darkest reaches of the Devil's Post Office. No one knows what happened to the letters. There is not a DEAD LETTER BOX in that post office!

The Matheson Cove

In the Shadow of the Devil's Post Office

by

Eva Nell Mull Wike, Ph.D.

TENNESSEE VALLEY
Publishing
2006

Published by:

       Tennessee Valley Publishing,
       P.O. Box 52527,
       Knoxville, Tennessee 37950-2527
       www.TVP1.com

Library of Congress Control Number: 2006902443

ISBN 1-932604-32-4

Book illustrations and cover design by Jim Wike.

∞ Dedication ∞

To the memory of my son, Joseph Howard Wike, &
To the memory of my nephew, Jason Donald Mull

"For wisdom will come into your heart, and
Knowledge will be pleasant to your soul" …

Proverbs 2:10

The Matheson Cove

In the Shadow of the Devil's Post Office

Contents

Part 1 Working on Two Hundred Years

Part 2 Dazzling Progress

List of Illustrations and Photographs

Acknowledgments

We have to reach back many decades in time to consider all the individuals who have made a contribution to our lives in the Matheson Cove. My daring to generate pages of manuscript about our parents and our ancestors is a bit overwhelming. But the lessons we learned from our parents, Joseph David Mull and Martha Jane Wimpey Mull, did not include how to give up when faced with challenging situations. Thus, I have plodded along, inspired by continuous encouragement from my many brothers and sisters. With a determined effort I have sought to weave our story into the beautiful tapestry of Appalachian History.

Spanning more than two hundred years of pioneering effort by these mountain dwellers, whom I call my people, I have attempted to 'do them justice' in this book. A never ending flow of meaningful notes provided by my siblings, Bennie Louise Mull Yaus, Ida Jane Mull Rowland, James Carl Mull and Donald Roger Mull, has filled me with a sense of empowerment.

The determination to write my first book, about folks whom I hold dear just seemed to be the right thing to do at this point in my life. Goodness knows that I have tried to follow, inter alie, the first rule of our household which was to 'always speak the truth!' Of course there are many endearing stories left untold. Those stories remain for another time and another author.

The list of contributors to this document must begin with my dear Aunt Mary Mease, who is so willing to tell, once more, those treasured stories of her life and times with her sister, Martha Jane; my cousin, Sarah Mease, who has searched untiringly for more details regarding our family; Uncle George Wimpey, who has left us with great coverage of the Wimpey family; our cousins, Jane Jensen and Sharon Wimpey Thurman, who have provided in-depth stories about the early lives of the Wimpey family. Jane's father, Uncle Carl Jensen, filled our imagination with great stories of faraway places when we were small children. The impact of those exciting stories upon me is immeasurable.

By way of our Uncle Johnny Mull, we have a revered link to our past, which Johnny eagerly shared in photographs and stories. Our cousin, Mary Nichols, provided many dates and detailed accounts about our ancestors. The genealogy information provided by my brother, David Levoan Mull and his wife, Donna Moncrief Mull, provides a tie to many of our people. Historical photographs were provided by my cousin, Jane Mease Cunningham, and her husband, Bob Cunningham.

Beyond my family, sources of inspiration for writing this book have been provided by many people. Foremost is my friend, Reba Ledford Rigsbee, who inspired me by sharing the story of her childhood in the Matheson Cove. Mary Fonda, Librarian at the Moss Memorial Library, provided me with historical documents. Opal Anderson Tiger shared her first-hand knowledge of how young folks use to write their letters to 'the Devil.' Opal and her hiking buddies walked many times to the Shewbird Mountain and placed their letters in the Devil's Post Office. Other folks who kindly shared their knowledge and photographs include Brenda Kay Ledford, Barbara Ledford Wright, Beth Jarrett Walton, Glenda Prater Murray, Carl Moore, Wayne and Carl Long, Tommy Moore, Ottie Faye Nelson Ashe, Clyta Russell Matheson and Howard Matheson.

My 'distant' cousin, Peggy Ann Wiggins Mahoney, has conveyed meaningful and pertinent facts to me, as we have hiked the ridges of Tennessee. She has willingly listened to me and advised me during this endeavor. Our 'connection' dates back to the early 1730's when Peggy's grandmother, Catharina Mull, and my grandfather, Peter Mull, lived as sister and brother in Burke County, North Carolina.

A grim and piteous incident relating to the exodus of the Cherokee Indians, actually took place in the pioneer home of Peggy's great-great grandparents, Margaret Deaver Wiggins and Abraham Wiggins. It was in their home on Alarka Creek that the great Cherokee leader, Tsali, was served his last meal. It has been called 'a simply act of kindness' provided by Margaret Wiggins. That fateful morning Tsali, his sons and brother were to give their lives so that one thousand other Cherokee Indians could remain in the mountains. After their meal, Abraham Wiggins had a brief prayer service for them. Unblindfolded, the condemned Indians then faced their executors.

Professional support during the writing of this book has come through editorial expertise provided by Chris Hackett and Lois Tomas. The illustrations created by my husband, James Seymour Wike, Sr., have provided the finishing touch to this document. Through Jim's endearing support, extraordinary dedication and artistic talent, I have found the inspiration to tell our story.

Prologue

T he branches that flow from the ancient Matheson family in the Loch Lomond region of the Scottish Highlands to the modern day Matheson are well documented. The name Matheson comes from the Gaelic MacMhathain meaning "Son of the Bear." Today the Chief of the Clan is Major Sir Fergus Matheson. Pictured above is his coat of arms.

As the name, "Son of the Bear" implies, the ancient Matheson clan was rugged and fought many battles along the windswept slopes of northern Scotland. The motto of the clan, Fac et spera (Do and hope), reflects the spirit of the clansmen. They have made a historic contribution in the Scottish Highlands and in many other regions of the world.

One example reveals how the Matheson clansmen fought for Donald, Lord of the Isles, at the battle of Harlaw in 1411. At that time, with a number of around 2,000 men, the clan Matheson was deemed as powerful as the MacKenzies. Losing that battle created disquietude; a prompt arrest by King James I at Inverness, Scotland, and the beheading of their chief in Edinburgh. Even though this was the final blow for the chief of the warriors, the chief ship remained in the Matheson family.

The battles continued to rage in the Highlands, during the 16th and 17th centuries. This was particularly so between the Matheson and Macdonald

Clans. Identified as belonging to the House of Buchanan, the Matheson name has become well known throughout the world.

When Christian MacKenzie Matheson gave birth to her son, Alexander Matheson, on December 14, 1741, she could have never imagined that he would become a 'world traveler.' Through his travels, he would influence the spreading of his people to many places in the world.

In Fodderty Parish of Easter-Ross, Scotland, Christian and her husband, Charles Matheson, would raise their son, Alexander. They also belonged to the House of Buchanan. It was here, on November 15, 1785, that Charles died at the age of 71. He is buried at Height of Inchrory, Scotland. Two years later, on March 4, 1787, Christian died at the age of 72. She is buried at Blairninich, Scotland.

Sometime about 1772, Alexander Matheson decided to depart his beloved homeland in the Scottish Highlands. Like many brave immigrants, he sailed into a harbor of the United States of America. According to historical documents, Alexander (d. 1832) was able to settle in Burke County, North Carolina, and served in the 8th Company of Militia. There he lived on property he had acquired by a land grant in 1789. This date is not exact, as many settlers lived on the land for a few years before applying for a land grant. He and his wife, Mary Miller (b. 06-12-1743), were also able to acquire property in Iredell County, NC. One of their sons, John Matheson (b. 1775) married Barbara McKenzie in 1798, and settled on 160 acres of land in Iredell County. John became a blacksmith and bought a lot in Statesville, NC, in 1803. Later (1880), he was listed in the records as a minister and a farmer.

The descendants of John and Barbara Matheson moved westward from Iredell County into Cherokee County, NC, during the mid 1800's. One of their sons, Marion Eli Matheson (b. 1804) and his wife, Anna Best Matheson (b. 1808; d. 1878) settled on a homestead on Clear Creek in Cherokee County, NC, in October, 1869. From census records of 1870, in Clay County, NC, Eli and Anna Best Matheson were some of the earliest settlers in the region of Clay County. They had seven children. One of these children, Elisha Dallas Matheson (b. 7-15-1844; d. 04-01-1926) married Martha Elizabeth Norwood (b. 08-30-1851; d. 01-30-1924) on February 23, 1871, in Clay County.

Dallas and Martha raised a family of three girls and three boys in the Matheson Cove. Their daughter, Minnie Lee Matheson (b. 8-18-1891; d. 10-16-1969) married Robert Lee 'Bob' Ledford in 1916, and moved back to the Matheson Cove in 1929.

According to a lecturer, Margie Prater (1996, in Clayton, GA), as early as 1844, Dallas Matheson owned 300 acres of land in the Matheson Cove. Prater stated, "Dallas was a learned man. He spoke with correct and distinct English. He read many books and so did his children."

Dallas was a knowledgeable farmer. His property included nearly one-half of the Shewbird Mountain. At the highest elevation he was able to grow fine peaches and apples. The fruit trees were above the frost line. Thus the fruit blossoms were never damaged by the killing frosts in the Cove. Dallas would transplant the wild huckleberry bushes to a lower elevation. Through this effort, he was able to provide other folks in the Cove access to the delicious blue berries in season.

Dallas's expertise extended to the harvesting of chestnuts and other edible wild fruits. He would punch a hole in the chestnuts before roasting them on his fireplace hearth. This would prevent the chestnuts from exploding during the roasting process.

There were many fine chestnut trees growing in the Matheson Cove during the early 1900's. Dallas had many kinds of apple trees. One kind was called 'black beauty.' It was such a deep red it was almost black. Another kind was the 'Ben Davis,' which was a light color with small streaks of red. It was white on the inside. There were others, such as the horse apple, hog sweet, red June, striped June, striped May, pumpkin apple, queen pippin, pound apple, and many others with no name.

Sadly, today the apple trees and the chestnut trees are no longer growing along the upper slopes of the Matheson Cove. The Shewbird Mountain stands yet as a 'sentinel.' The mountain should serve today as a reminder of the dutiful respect Elisha Dallas Matheson exhibited while living in the Cove.

Author's Notes

Through the writing of this book, *The Matheson Cove – In the Shadow of the Devil's Post Office*, I have sought to capture the beauty of birth, the agony of losing a loved one, the true dedication of my parents to their eleven children and their never ending faith in God. It was through their faith and dedication that they were able to make a life for their children in the Cove. While weaving stories provided by my brothers and sisters through my own recollections; I have written this book with the utmost appreciation and devotion to our dearly beloved parents.

The isolation and hard-times, as revealed in the photographs, may simply be the reasons we can call ourselves strong mountain folks. Running deeply through my soul is a determination that can not be reflected in a photograph or a paragraph. If I can capture this resolve and give it to my grand children, then I will have lived a good life.

Part 1
Working on Two Hundred Years

Chapter 1

The Winter of 1838

My Maternal Great-Grandmother

Our family putting down permanent roots in the Matheson Cove, in the shadow of the Devil's Post Office, seems to be a natural link to our distant past. This perception is based on my early childhood memories of stories we were told about our maternal great-grandmother, Matilda 'Minnie' Little. Our mother would often share details about her grandmother's life in the majestic mountains over in North Georgia.

As mama would prepare to cook cornbread in our Dutch oven; gathering the hot coals from the fireplace; she would once again begin to tell us more details about her grandmother, Minnie. It was a sad story! It began when Minnie was a young girl. She was able to hide out in a cave near Track Rock, Georgia. Somehow she survived that terrible winter of 1838.

A hundred years before I was born, my great-grandmother, Minnie, had sought refuge under the harshest conditions. I could not imagine having the courage to even go near the Devil's Post Office, a cave hidden away in the Shewbird Mountain. The Shewbird stands like a sentinel behind our house in the Matheson Cove. In my mind, the Devil's Post Office is a foreboding place!

1

As a child, I imagined the Devil's Post Office holding many dark secrets of times long ago. Daddy told us that young folks actually use to write letters to 'the Devil' and place those letters in the dark reaches of the Shewbird Mountain. That fact scares me even today! But back in 1838, Minnie Little was not afraid of the cavernous mountains over in Georgia. That dreadful winter, she found refuge when her people were being driven away from their homeland. She was determined to live out her days in the place of her birth!

Back in 1830, when the United States Congress passed the "Indian Removal Act," Minny's fate seemed sealed. In spite of the ruling handed down by Supreme Court Justice John Marshall; that the "Indian Removal Act" was invalid; the United States President, Andrew Jackson, ignored the decision. The Act argued that "no state could achieve proper culture, civilization, and progress, as long as Indians remained within its boundaries."

Minny and her people were living in the north end of Georgia which was called the "Cherokee Strip." The Cherokee Tribe continued to occupy this region until 1832. The region was then taken away from them and the land was given away by lottery. There was no hope that Justice John Marshall or other noted statesmen, such as Henry Clay, could stop the tortuous journey in which so many people would perish.

When the "Removal Treaty of New Echota" was signed by the Cherokee Treaty Party in 1835, times grew even darker for Minny and her people. With this treaty, President Jackson then had the legal document he needed to remove the Cherokee Indians. The discovery of gold, the desire for land by the white settlers, and the determination by the 'ruling' political leaders all allowed for the removal of the Cherokee Nation.

This process has been called 'one of the saddest episodes of our nation's history.' Today the removal appears to summarize what was wrong with American policy at that time. The claim by President

Jackson that his policy was founded on a humanitarian platform seems like a mockery. He never expressed regret for the appalling disaster. Of course he was no longer President of the United States. Returning home, to *The Hermitage*, he remained silent. Perhaps his silence said enough!

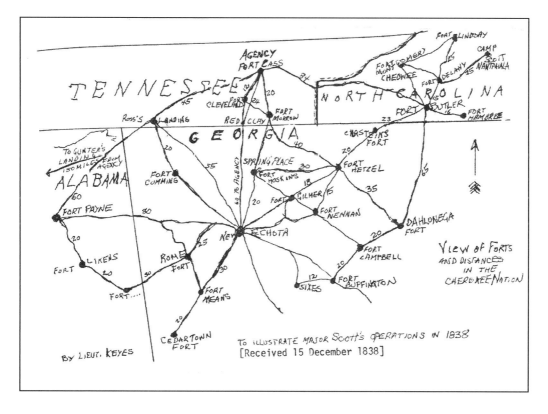

Map #1. Forts established for General Scott's operations, 1838.

It is difficult to imagine how such a brutal decimation of one quarter of the Cherokee Nation could have occurred. Especially so, since only a few decades before our country had been founded on the premise "that all men are created equal, and that they are endowed by their Creator with certain unalienable rights, among these the right to life, liberty and the pursuit of happiness."

Great effort was put forth by many people to challenge the removal process. About 15,000 Cherokees signed a petition asking the United

States Congress to invalidate the Treaty of Echota. On April 23, 1838, Ralph Waldo Emerson wrote to President Martin Van Buren, urging him not to inflict "so vast an outrage upon the Cherokee Nation." When the United States Senate ratified the Removal Treaty by one vote, many people voiced their opposition. General John Wool resigned his command in protest, thus delaying the removal process.

As the May 23, 1838 deadline for voluntary removal approached, President Martin Van Buren ordered Major General Winfield Scott into Cherokee Territory. Scott was to use whatever force required in moving the Cherokees west. Principal Chief John Ross made an urgent appeal to delay the removal until fall. The request was granted. Somehow Minny was able to escape the horrible march during the winter of 1838, and became my maternal great-grandmother.

Illustration 1. Minny Little hiding from the soldiers.

It saddens me to know that Minny and Asa Thomason's names are the only two names which appear on the records for my grandmother Wimpey's family. These marriage documents (01-13-1857), in the Clarksville, Georgia Courthouse records, indicate that Minny Little's nationality is 'unknown.' With great reverence to the Cherokee Nation, I hereby declare that my great-grandmother, Matilda 'Minny' Little, will no longer be classified as 'unknown!'

Today this "Nunna dual Tsun" or *The Place Where They Cried* remains as a dark line through our history. The curtain was closed on the great Cherokee Nation. During the march, pioneers stood and cried as they watched the piteous procession of Cherokee Indians moving along the trail which stretched for 2,200 miles.

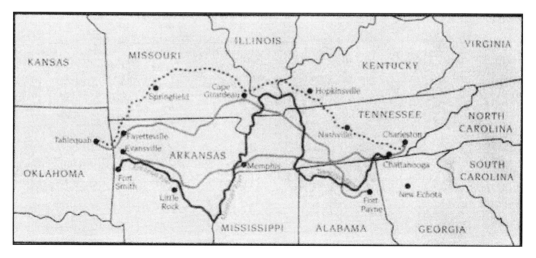

Map # 2. The Trail of Tears route ---- by land __ by water, 1987.

A 1984 scholarly demographic study estimated that a total of 8,000 people died as a result of the Trail of Tears. In 1987, the United States Congress designated the Trail of Tears a National Historical Trail.

My Fraternal Grandparents

From a time far back, I knew that my father's ancestors had settled in North Carolina, in the 1700's. Early records reveal that our forefather, Christophel Moll, was born in the west-central region of Germany, known as Hesse (German: Hessen). Hesse is a hilly countryside surrounded by a mountain chain called the Odenwald. The river Rhine borders this region on the southwestern side without flowing through Hesse. The search for religious freedom and escape from conflicts, that were rife between Lutherans and Calvinists, brought many immigrants to America, during the 1700's.

Christophel arrived in the United States, September 10, 1731, on "The Pennsylvania Merchant." In the German language, the word Moll is a technical term in music, meaning 'minor.' His name was later changed to Mull. In the Scottish Gaelic language, the word Mull is a geographical term meaning promontory or headland. Christophel's family members were active in the Goshenhoppen Reformed Church which stands today, one mile west of East Greenville, Montgomery County, PA.

Within Burke and Catawba Counties in NC, our ancestors were described as 'prominent families with great wealth.' Christophel and his wife, Anna Catharina, had three sons and one daughter. Christophel was known to have owned more than a thousand acres of land in Rowan County, NC. This county was formed in 1753, and was the most westerly county in North Carolina, at that time.

Their son, Peter Mull (b. 1735/36; d. 10-29-1805), would become my fraternal grandfather six generations later. Grandfather Peter served as High Sheriff in Burke County, NC. He married Barbara A. Cline (b. bef 1740; d. 1836/37) and had a son named John (b. 1760; d. 10-12-1812). John and Catherine Weidner (Whitener) (b. 1756; d. 05-02-1839) were married about 1781, and had eight children; one being Henry Mull (b. 04-08-1787; d. 03-24-1857). On February 9, 1809, Henry married Mary Hull (b. 1792; d. aft 1860) and one of their children, Harrison Mull (b. 1816; d. 1849) would become our direct linage to the brave immigrants, who sailed on the ship "The Pennsylvania Merchant," back in September, 1731.

Our fraternal great-great-grandfather, Harrison Mull, died at age 33, while attempting to ford a river with his team of horses in Burke County, NC. He is buried at Mull's Chapel in Catawba County, NC.

After Harrison's death, his young widow, Annie Mosteller Mull (b. 01-1825), was left alone to raise their four children. Annie was strong and tried to carry on without Harrison. Her children included a daughter Adeline (b. 07-06-1844; d. 01-12-1916) and three sons, Harvey (b. 07-02-1842; d. 11-22-1914), George Munroe (b. 01-15-1847; d. 04-08-1928) and Franklin (b. bet 05-02-1840/49; d. 05-22-1926).

Annie's holdings included much land and property. However, the Civil War would change her way of life and render the Confederate money worthless. After the Civil War, Annie's brother, Peter Mosteller, chose to leave Burke County, and settle in a community called Tusquittee (meaning 'The Rafters'), in the most westerly Cherokee Indian Territory in NC. Peter and his wife, Sarah Mull Mosteller, were the first settlers in the Tusquittee area when the new Indian Territory became open for settlement. Soon afterwards, Annie chose to sell her land and follow her brother westward.

With much strength and fortitude, Annie loaded her three younger children and few belongings in a wagon and headed west. Annie's trip took many days, with a team of horses and children in tow. She would camp at night and travel by day. The roads leading to Tusquittee were just ruts and sometimes very difficult to travel. Somehow Annie and her children survived the journey. She was resolute and able to make a life for her family in the community of Tusquittee. Annie's oldest son, Frank, was already married (aft 1862) to Myra Settlemyer (b. 03-1847; d. 08-12-1916), a native Tennessean. He soon followed his family to Tusquittee. There he and Myra raised a family of six children in the mid 1800's. Frank and Myra would become my fraternal great-grandparents.

Photo 1. Great-grandfather, Frank Mull, circa, 1910.
(Courtesy of Mary McClure Nichols, 2006)

One of their sons, Calvin Monroe Mull (b. 10-30-1872; d. 11-24-1954), was to become my grandfather. On March 15, 1896, Calvin Monroe married Ida Lee Smith (b. 01-17-1877; d. 12-18-1964) at the residence of the Reverend David Prewitt. For the ceremony, they stood on a large hearth stone in the Prewitt cabin. Many years later, the beautiful hearth stone from the Prewitt's home place was carefully selected to be used in the construction of the Moss Memorial Church on Tusquittee.

Today the stone can be viewed at the lower left corner of the main entrance to the Church. This stone along with thousands more were collected from many home sites across the valleys to be used in the building of the Church. Fortunately, the stonemasons took pride in their work and exhibited great sensitivity by preserving the identity of this stone for our family.

Photo 2. Stone on which Grandma and Grandpa stood, 1896.
(Courtesy of Johnny Mull, 2006.)

Calvin and Ida raised a family on Tusquittee, beginning in the vicinity of Big Tuni. Their first child was a girl, Bessie Emmaline (b. 11-1898, d. 1979), named in honor of her maternal grandmother. My father, Joseph David Mull, was born to them on February 18, 1900. In September of the following year their second daughter was born and they named her Lula "Lou" (b: 09-04-1901; d. 05-10-1996). Their daughter, Lillie was born February 4, 1908, and passed away July 19, 1992, exactly one month after her brother, Joseph David, had died. Lastly, three more sons would be born to Ida and Calvin. James Sullivan (Jimmy) was born on November 29, 1912, and died on October 30, 2001. Jessie was born on October 8, 1915. He died December 16, 1930, at the age of fifteen because of an ear infection.

Photo 3. Calvin and Ida Mull with children
l. to r. **Joe, Lillie, Jimmy, Jessie and Lou, 1915.**
(Courtesy of Mary McClure Nichols, 2006.)

That winter of 1930, must have been rough for Ida and Calvin. All the sad details were woven into the childhood events my daddy would later recall, time after time, as he told us about his younger days. In daddy's words, "It just didn't seem right that 'Poor Little Jessie' had to die so young." But his youngest brother, Johnny, born May 30, 1922, brought much joy to all members of Joe's family. Today, Uncle Johnny eagerly shares precious stories of times long passed.

Back when daddy was born, at the turn of the century, life was not much easier than in the old days of the 1800's. If folks could raise a successful crop of corn and vegetables, they would be able to feed their cattle and preserve food for the winter months. With a few chickens and a good milk cow they could provide most of their needs. Being able to hunt wild game added a fair supplement to their diet.

Cutting firewood and just trying to stay warm during the long winter nights seemed to be a big part of their daily effort. My daddy told us, "Many a time I woke in the night and brushed snow off my bedcovers. The old log house could get mighty airy and cold as the night wore on into the dawn!"

A tradition of sharing stories and staying in touch with ancestral history was a very important part of a young person's upbringing. In this isolated region of North Carolina, there were no cars, no electricity, and no books except the Holy Bible. Hard times just seemed to be a way of life. But families stayed close and shared their memories by the fireside. Not many folks knew how to read or write. But my daddy learned to tell meaningful stories at an early age. He wanted so much to get a good education. His love of learning stayed with him all his life.

As children, we sat around the fireside and listened to daddy tell us stories of his boyhood days. One of my favorite is the story about the day when he and grandpa Mull got up real early one morning and 'hoofed it' all the way into town. Hayesville was about ten miles from their home place. Grandpa had heard that an automobile was coming to town that very day. They were so eager to witness it. In daddy's words, "It was a sight to see! The car was right there and I got to see it move about. The car made a loud noise! The horses and mules around the 'Square' had to be restrained."

Illustration 2. First car (1913 Ford Roadster) in Hayesville, 1914.

Grim stories also filled my father's childhood life. One such story grandpa Calvin had told his young son, Joe, dealt with a hanging grandpa had witnessed. After the hanging, the rope was cut into short pieces and thrown into the crowd. They never knew why the man was hung. Such gruesome stories were a reality of life back in those days.

But ghost stories were grandpa's 'specialty.' Back when I was a youngster, folks claimed Calvin Monroe Mull could tell a ghost story that would make the hair stand up on the back of your neck! The warm fire burning in that big stone fireplace could not keep you from shivering when grandpa got to the scariest part of his ghost story. Even the coon dogs snoring near the fireplace and the squeaking of grandma's old rocking chair just seemed to add to the ghostly aura. It did not take much to make a young fellow want to climb right up into grandpa's lap to ward off the ghosts and howling winds.

The sceerest ghost story grandpa ever told us wus about this here ole woman who wus out hoen in her gyarden late one afternoon. Dusksome wus jest about fallen and all of a sudden she noticed sumem in the loamy soil. She fixed to put her hoe to hit and hit kinda of leapt beyant her hoe like hit jes mought be alive. Hit shore didn't look like no sech a thang she'd ever seed be for now. Then agin, hit kinda reminded her of her grandpa's BIG TOE!

Welser, this desided her she mought orta pick hit up and hev a closer gander at hit. And tha's zxactly what she done! Yesiree! When she picked that thar thang up and tuk a closer gander, hit peered to be a good piece of meat.

In a thoughty maner she sez, "By Ned. I's a good mind to jest take hit in the hause and throw hit in that thare stew I ben a fixen fur grandpa aw day! Hit jest mought make that stew taste xtra spe shal!"

Ignoren the call of the scrooch owl; she went rat inside and drapped that BIG TOE in that thar pot of stew. With that, she jest added to her FADAL MIS TAKE of first apicken that dang thang up in her gyarden. Grandpa went rat ahead and ate up all his stew that night. Hit wuz moughty good stew as fur as he could tell. But the night wuz'nt yet over! The ole woman was goen die! Hit goes odd with me, but the rest of the story is too skeerey to tell.

Grandma Mull never told us scary stories. To me, she always seemed to have a sad look about her, like she had known lots of sorry. For sure her mama had known much sorry. My great-grandma, Emmaline Perry had lost her husband during the Civil War. Later, she would marry Nicholas Smith and have two sons, Bob and Tom. My grandma Mull was born in 1877, and great-grandma Emmaline raised my grandma all by herself.

My daddy use to tell us that his mama loved music and dancing when she was young. Grandma taught daddy to pick the banjo, when he was age five. She could play a banjo good! She was proud of her brother, Tom Smith, who had won a World Exhibition Competition in banjo picking, held in Chicago, back before the turn of the century.

Breaking Away

In the fall of 1923, when Johnny was just a baby, Joseph David decided he would leave Tusquittee and go north. He and his friend, Paul Moore, made plans to drive up to Canton, Ohio, to seek employment in the steel mills. Daddy cranked up his Model T-Ford and they started their journey along the rough roads leading out of North Carolina across the Great Smoky Mountains. Travel conditions in the high mountains were not exactly ideal in the fall of 1923.

In later years daddy would relate how he and Paul struggled just to get through the mountains. The muddy ruts crossing the Smokies were a real challenge! "With great determination," daddy said, "we went as far as we could go until we got stuck in the mud. Then we backed up, revved the engine and hit the ruts as hard as we could to go a little farther! We kind of lost count but I believed we had twenty-three flat tires during the trip. Those tires were mighty thin! We used news-papers to line the inside of the tires to protect the inner tubes. Finally, after five days we arrived in Canton."

Daddy was able to find work at the Timken Roller Bearing Company and his salary was about fifty cent an hour. That was good money compared to what he could earn back home in the mountains! Of course grandma thought Joe would never return home. But in the spring of 1924, she received a letter from her dear son. She could read between the lines just how much Joe longed to see everybody back home.

1825 Garfield Ave.
Canton, Ohio
Feb. 25, 24

Monday even.

Dear Mother,

I read your letter today and was pleased to hear from you all and to know that you was all well. This leaves me well and hope this will find you all well. I am still working. I haven't work but 3 hours today. They got something wrong with the machines this morning and we are off till in the morning. Well it is mighty cold today. Snowing every day. I am liking here fine. I don't know jus when I will leave here. I may stay a long time and I may not. Jus when I take a notion I will leave. I would like to see little Johnie now. I guess he is talking bye now. I got a letter from Peed and Bessie today. I would like to be at the Singing School at Chigger Hill. I would like to hear some good singing. Now I haven't heard any since I have been here – that is good singing. I heard that Arvil and Donie was married. Well I can't think of anything to write. I will close. Answer soon.

Your son,
Joe

It was not long until Joe bid Canton, Ohio, his 'first adieu.' Returning to his family and 'Little Johnie' was a happy time for him. But in a few months he would leave again for the cotton mills of Spartanburg, South Carolina. He was approaching twenty-five years of age and was determined to seek his fortune far from Tusquittee.

Photo 4. Joseph David Mull, Spartanburg, SC, circa 1925.
(Courtesy of Eva Nell Mull Wike, 2006.)

Daddy was able to find work in a cotton mill down in Spartanburg, SC, and enjoyed his time in the flatland. But his heart was back in the ridges and valleys of Tusquittee. He kept recalling that beautiful young girl he had seen over on Qualla, a few years back. What if he stayed in South Carolina? What if that beautiful girl married someone else? Well, that was not going to happen!

Joe returned in early 1926, to his home on Tusquittee. He found his little brother, Johnny, had grown. Otherwise, things seemed to have not changed since he went away. His mama and papa were still able to work and take care of themselves. But he knew that would not be the case as the years passed. Daddy wanted to stay close by and help his folks. He just could not become a city dweller. The mountains were too much a soulful part of his being. It was here he would raise a large family of his own and live out his days in the mountains of Clay County.

I remember in the early 1950's, when we would visit grandma and grandpa. It seemed daddy would always be 'worried about papa.' Somehow, in these sad conversations and visits we learned how to turn loose of folks we loved. In the late autumn of 1954, grandpa weakened and was unable to walk.

As a child, sleeping upstairs in our house, I could hear daddy talk quietly to mama about grandpa's condition. Once I heard him say, "Papa has taken his death bed." Later on, daddy began sitting up all night with his papa. He insisted that grandpa not be left alone to die. Finally, one day I overheard daddy tell mama, "When I left papa this morning, I could hear he had the 'death rattles.'" I had never heard those words. I wondered how 'death rattles' sounded. Sadly, I thought, "No more of grandpa's stories!"

I was a sophomore in high school when grandpa passed away. It seemed grandma was mighty lonesome, all alone in that big old house. Of course she still had her coon dogs. She loved her dogs! She seemed to do fairly well for several years. But one day I heard daddy talking to mama regarding what his brother, Jimmy, had told him.

It seemed Jimmy had gone to visit his mama. Sitting in her rocker by the fireside, grandma was able to greet Jimmy. But when he asked her how she was doing her response did not make sense. Daddy's voice had the same worried tone as back when he would talk about his papa being low. It was not long until grandma had 'taken to her death bed.' Daddy and other folks began their sitting with grandma around the clock. Somehow we accepted grandma's passing a little easier. Maybe we were learning some hard lessons about living and dying.

Later on Uncle Jimmy was working and cleaning out things in the house. There he found a long lost book with the words 'Joe Mull's Book' written on about page 50. The covers of the book had been torn away and the first fifty pages were missing. My dear Uncle Jimmy brought the book down to daddy and said, "Joe, I believe this is your book." Daddy was a little embarrassed and somewhat amused at the condition of the book. Being the shy man he was, he kindly thanked Jimmy and hid the book away in a shoebox.

More than twenty years after he had received the tattered book, he showed it to me. He said, "I don't want to throw the book away. It was my only book besides the Bible. But it sure is a pitiful excuse for a history book. Do you reckon I could just give it to you?"

Fighting back my tears, I said, "Daddy I would love to have the book! It would mean so much to me." He kind of grinned, as if he were thinking, "I knew Eva Nell would take it off my hands!"

I took the book to Nashville, and searched in many libraries for a history book like daddy's book. Finally I located one at Vanderbilt University Library and copied the first fifty pages. I took the pages and daddy's book to an antique bookbinding store. When I asked the owner if he could restore my daddy's book, he just laughed at me and said, "That book has seen better days!" I responded, "And so have I! How much will you charge me? It is for my 86 year old daddy."

After getting the book restored to mint condition, I took it back to daddy. I was going to give it to him for a Christmas gift. Of course he would not take the book. He said, "Honey, that book is yours! It's much too fine for me!" Today that green leather bound book, with the gold letters 'JOSEPH DAVID MULL' engraved on the front cover, occupies a very special place in my heart and home. His picture and his parent's picture complete the setting.

Photo 5. Grandma and Grandpa Mull, circa 1950.
(Courtesy of Ida Jane Mull Rowland, 2006.)

Now to the final story about my grandpa Mull! So many times daddy told us about an accident in which grandpa nearly got killed. A long time ago, it seemed he was taking a short cut to get home one day. As he entered a fenced area where a 'mean' bull was resting he knew he was in dangerous territory. Getting closer to the other side of the pasture, he thought he was home free, but not so! The angry bull charged him and gored him almost to death. Grandpa was able to push his entrails back into his abdomen, roll under the barbed wire fence and somehow walked home. My grandpa Mull was a brave man!

My Grandparents

My grandparents were strong folks.
They followed plows and bent to toil.
They moved through fields sowing seed.
They touched the earth and crops grew.
They were full of sturdiness and singing.
Yes, my grandparents were strong.

Adapted from "My Grandmothers" Margaret Walker, 2005.

It seems good just to hold on to recollections from way back when we traveled by wagon on our regular Sunday afternoon visits up to Tusquittee. One of my favorite things was how we could always find a jar of 'sourwood' honey sitting on grandma's kitchen table. She and grandpa had so many honey bee gums a body could get stung just walking passed all of them. If we arrived at grandma's house early enough we might get one of her good biscuits. Those biscuits smothered in honey were mighty good eating!

Recently, I visited my Uncle Johnny Mull, up on Tusquittee. He said daddy was right about his mama! "Mama surely loved mountain music and dancing." Recalling earlier years, "One thing my mama and papa loved to do was have a party when papa's brother, John, and his family came over visiting from Andrews. Of course we didn't have a telephone back then, so they would just hang white sheets on the clothes line. That way everybody passing by would know there was going to be music and dancing that night. Yeah, my mama loved to dance!"

When Johnny was about three years old, his mama and papa were having a dance at their house. His mama had laid him down to sleep on a bed in the middle room and they were dancing in the back room. Well, it seemed that some fine lady had placed her fox fur on the bed where 'Little Johnny' was sleeping. He woke up and in the dim lamplight he could see a fox head with two beady eyes staring straight at him. Johnny said, "I started screaming and mama came a running. She tried to tell me it wasn't real. That didn't matter to me! I yelled, 'Just get me out of here!'"

My Maternal Grandparents

How far into the past must one travel, by the written word, to learn just how brave and enduring their grandparents were in the early times? It seems perfectly natural that my maternal grandfather's folks would have settled in the remote region of North Georgia. Granddad, William Isaac Wimpey, was born in Indian Territory called 'Arkaqua' on July 31, 1878. He was the fourth child of William Frank Wimpey and Sarah Melinda Collins Wimpey.

As a young man, Will could see his mother's cabin clinging to a slope just on the other side of the creek. He had built his own log cabin from logs he had hewed with an adze. As Will 'followed the plow' in the fertile earth, he was in harmony with nature. In winter the soil (Arkaqua Loam) which he tilled, would be replenished when the hard winter rains flooded the small farm.

My maternal grandmother, Lula Bell Jane Thomason, was born May 29, 1879, in Arkagua, Georgia. She was the daughter of Minny Little Thomason and Asa Thomason. Jane and William were married September 2, 1900, in Arkaqua. A few years after they were married they realized the small farm would not support their extended families.

In 1903, Will and Jane packed their belongings into their wagon and left their home place. Their journey, with their young sons, Frank and Onas, was a most difficult seventeen hours of travel. Arriving in the late evening, Jane and Will found refuge in a small church near Hayesville.

Photo 6. 'Restored' Fort Hembree Baptist Church.
(Courtesy of James Seymour Wike, Sr., 2006.)

These difficult times were later recounted, 'how the warm hospitality extended to them by the members of the church was so appreciated.' During the services Jane and Will would sit quietly with their two young sons, in the back of the church.

In just a few weeks, Will and Jane were settled into a small cabin in the Morgan Cove, just off Peckerwood Road. Drawing on his earlier 'work experience' in the field of moon shining; granddad soon began to increase his take-home-pay through his knowledge of chemistry and copper stills. The determinate which brought about his great success was his acquaintance with the Mostellers, who lived in the Upper Tusquittee Valley. These folks were making a living in this 'field of corn.' Fortunately, granddad had brought his beautiful copper distillery with him from Georgia. Thus, he continued his profession in what some folks, at that time, called 'bootlegging.'

In a short time Will and Jane moved to the Mosteller Place on Tuni Creek, just across from the Morgan Cove. Here my mother, Martha Jane, was born on April 22, 1907. As children, we use to ask mama about grandpa's 'bootlegging' and she would never share any details with us. Neither she nor her sister, Mary Linda Ann Matilda (b. 08-24-1904) had any part of such forbidden activities

Uncle George Wimpey (b. 1916; d. 1998) told how granddad became friends with Rob Mosteller and soon partners in the bootlegging business. One well know story which Uncle George related, is about granddad's close call with the Revenue Agents:

"Will Wimpey and Duke Stamey were in a dense Ivy thicket riveting a mash tank when the agents crept up to within a few feet before being detected. Duke was inside the tank holding a dolly while Will headed the rivets from the outside. With no time to warn Duke, who couldn't have escaped anyway, Will dived headlong into the underbrush and clambered out of reach, making his escape. Unaware of the man inside, one of the Agents struck the tank with his pickax and was both surprised and amused when Duke rose up out of the tank and exclaimed, "Will, you've knocked a hell of a hole in this thing!" Duke went to prison without revealing the identity of his accomplice. Will supplied Duke with personal needs while he was incarcerated."

Illustration 3. Will and Duke at work on the 'Still,' circa 1910.

As the years passed, the family moved to Fires Creek, in 1912, and to Downings Creek, in 1914. In the Downings Creek community the family worked hard on the larger farm and attended the Oak Forest Church. Even so, granddad continued 'restoring' stills and supplementing his income with his distillery activities. Business was good because the Revenue Agents frequently damaged the beautiful copper stills grandpa had made for folks. Grandma was mighty worried and anxious about the risks grandpa was taking by continuing his moonshine business.

One day it happened! Grandpa was caught red-handed making a still and grandma's worst fears would come to pass. Grandpa was tried and had to serve one year in prison for violating the law. Grandma was left with eight children under the age of thirteen to care for during that year.

Photo 7. Will and Jane with children, *l. to r.* **Martha, Mary, Taft, Ella Vee, Bennie Lee, Jim, Onas and Frank, circa, 1913.**
(Courtesy of David L. Mull, 2006.)

Jane and the children worked hard to preserve food and gather feed for the farm animals. That winter things were mighty scarce and there was little to spare for the children. According to Uncle George, this experience left its mark on his mother. Her suffering did not go unnoticed by grandpa when he came home from prison. He would 'turn over a new leaf' and become a better man! His upright way of living and setting a good example for his children became the focus of his life.

In 1920, the family moved to Qualla. Grandpa assumed the management of the County Home. He got paid twenty dollars a month for each pauper who stayed at the Home. The County Home was situated on two hundred acres of land. My mother's happiest childhood memories seem to be centered on this time and place. Grandma, Aunt Mary and mama spent their days working hard. They would prepare food and keep the County Home nice for the paupers.

Grandma would spin wool to make yarn. Then she would make socks for the members of her own family. Mama seemed please to wear 'home made' stockings to school.

Photo 8. Grandma and Grandpa Wimpey, circa 1945.
(Courtesy of Ida Jane Rowland, 2006.)

In mama's words, "Mother was an awful good cook and grew most all our vegetables in her garden. She could knit, dye and make pretty things for us to wear. She could make the best teacakes!"

Mama liked to tell us about how much grandpa loved to sing. When he was 'working' over the mountain, she could hear him singing as he came home. "We knew his voice and knew that daddy would be home soon. Your dad means a lot to you, especially if you get to stay with him until you are grown. A favorite song of his was 'What a Friend We Have.'"

What a Friend We Have
(C. C. Converse, 1868 & Joseph Scriven, 1855)

1   What a friend we have in Jesus,
    all our sin and griefs to bear!
    What a privilege to carry
    everything to God in Prayer!
    Oh what peace we often forfeit,
    Oh what needless pain we bear,
    all because we do not carry
    everything to God in prayer.

2. Have we trials and temptations?
    Is there trouble anywhere?
    We should never be discouraged;
    take it to the Lord in prayer.
    Can we find a friend so faithful
    who will all our sorrows share?
    Jesus knows our every weakness;
    take it to the Lord in prayer.

3. Are we weak and heavy laden,
    cumbered with a load of care?
    Precious Savior, still our refuge,
    take it to the Lord in prayer.
    Do thy friends despise, forsake thee?
    Take it to the Lord in prayer!
    In his arms he'll take and shield thee,
    thou will find a solace there.

With the utmost respect and admiration, mama would often declare, "My daddy was a good man! He and my mother met for the first time on a mountain hike. My mother was breaking off little sticks from a bush and tossing them at dad. Dad asked her why she was throwing the twigs. She replied, 'I want to walk down the ridge with you!'"

This is such a pure and beautiful memory about my grandparents. An endearing recollection which daddy often related to us dealt with the very first time he saw my mother. This moment occurred when daddy was working in the forest near the County Home. "I saw a pretty young girl as she was carrying a pail of milk toward her house. At that moment I thought, "That's the girl I want to marry!" He often declared, "I think I fell in love with her at that very first glimpse!" This was unbeknownst to Martha Jane. It would be a long time before she learned of Joseph David's intent.

On Saturday nights Mary, Martha and all their brothers and sisters would party at the County Home. Friends and neighbors would gather under the big white pines in the yard to sing, make music and tell stories. Often the paupers would join in the singing. Other events that brought folks together were corn shuckings and socials. During a corn shucking, if a boy found a red ear of corn this could result in a kiss from his favorite girlfriend.

My Aunt Mary, who still lives on Qualla, at the age of 101 years, recalls their home to be filled with laughter, love and singing. A story she tells about mama is, "Martha use to love to rock the twins in a cradle which dad had built." The twins were Ollie Ella Vee and Mollie Bennie Lee Wimpey.

Just recently, Aunt Mary shared a very special memory about how the twins got their names. It seems that grandma Wimpey; after having delivered the twins; was just a little overcome with the idea of naming the twins. She expressed her concern to the attending physician. She exclaimed, "I've just never thought about naming twins!" The doctor replied, "I can help you choose names, if you like!" With a sigh of relief, grandma replied, "I sure could use some help with naming them!" The doctor quickly named Ella Vee after his wife and Bennie Lee after his daughter.

One of my favorite childhood stories mama told us was how she and her dear sister, Mary Matilda, would travel by ox-drawn cart from the Arkaqua home place to Downings Creek. Their Uncle Tom Wimpey would be driving the ox cart or the ox might be driving them, depending on Uncle Tom's sobriety. They would travel on the old trading route that had been cleared many years earlier by the Cherokee Indians and the 'Unicoi' traders.

Once when Martha and Mary were about six and ten years old, they were riding along with Uncle Tom. Suddenly he FELL out of the cart! They had to help him back in the cart and were then able to continue their long twenty mile journey. As they were riding through the town of Hayesville, Uncle Tom told them, "Get down in the cart and hide! You don't want to be seen riding with me! Somebody will think you're drunk!" This made Aunt Mary mad. She insisted Uncle Tom stop the cart and let her get out. Mama just got down in the cart and hid so no one would see her riding with Uncle Tom.

Such details always amazed me as to grandma's trust in Uncle Tom's capacity to get them through the rugged mountain trails. But my childhood recollections of Uncle Tom are filled with laughter and good cheer. When he would visit us he was always quick to sing a song or dance a little jig, right there in our front room. He was a lot like grandpa Wimpey.

Grandpa was always smiling, ready to talk and tell a funny story. He loved his grandchildren. As a greeting to the little children, he would be quick to lift them to 'the joist' and laugh with them. My son Jimmy, who was born in 1961, actually had the good fortune to visit with grandpa once. Of course grandpa lifted Jimmy up to 'the joist.' That was the last time we got to visit with grandpa Wimpey. He died in 1963.

A Guiding Light

There is an old mountain saying over in the hills of Tennessee: "A tall woman casts a long shadow!" Well, as far as I am concerned, my mother, my grandmothers, and my great-grandmothers have cast long shadows across my life. Their way of living, as Appalachian womenfolk, is a light for me even in the darkest hour.

Chapter 2

Courtship and Ceremony with T. C. Moore

In the early 1900's the Morgan Cove was a remote, sparsely settled region in Clay County, where my maternal grand parents lived. It was in this cove that my Aunt Mary Linda Matilda Wimpey was born August 24, 1904. In 1906, granddad Wimpey moved his family to the Mosteller Place on Tuni Creek. On April 22, 1907, my mother, Martha Jane, was born there. As grandpa Wimpey continued his bootlegging business, grandma Wimpey tried to provide her growing family with a good Christian upbringing.

My mother often related her childhood memories to us, which seemed to always centered around her sister, Mary Matilda. These were pleasant memories which brought laughter to my mother and to Aunt Mary. Back when mama was still living, nothing would please me more than to take her for a visit to Aunt Mary's on Qualla. Just the least inquiry would get them talking and recalling memories from their early childhood years.

Perhaps the best times were in the early 1920's, when the family had moved to the County Home on Qualla. Attending school was much easier then as they lived closer to the school and could walk home for lunch. Mama was about thirteen years old and wanted very much to do well and stay in school. But a harsh, 'red-headed' teacher made things too rough for mama and she became discouraged. At age fourteen, she declared "I will just stay home and help mother and dad with all the work on the farm. I will never marry!"

Thus, 'Scottie Bode' as my grandpa called my mother, entered her later teenage years helping her mother and father on the farm. Some of her favorite tasks involved working outside with her dad. They rode horses together, laughed and enjoyed those special years together.

According to mama, "It was great to work along side my brothers and help with the farm work. We traveled to church in a wagon. We were the only family who was able to 'travel by wagon' in the valley! Being a teenager was fun, but of course there were sad times." Mama recalls, "Like when we lost Onas, at only 15 years of age. He died of an eye infection. The doctor came to see him but he couldn't save dear Onas. It was his time to die!"

It was about this time in her life, that mama got the notion to go out dating. She explained, "For dates we usually went to church. But sometimes we just went riding in the buggy! My favorite times were when I would double date with my good friend Eula (Mease) Arwood."

However, when mama was about nineteen years old my daddy decided to make his intentions known to the beautiful young Martha Jane Wimpey! "After church, one Sunday afternoon," mama told us, "Joe David and his friend approached me and my friend, Miss Eula." It seems Joe David invited the two fair ladies to go for a Sunday afternoon ride in the buggy. On the surface, this seemed like a usual event for my mama. But you will recall, in her early teens she had declared, "I will never marry!" She had no intentions of getting serious with a young man! No sir!

Well, in a few weeks, my daddy made another call on Miss Martha. This time she declined the invitation to go for a ride in the rumble seat of his friend's auto. She was not impressed with the auto ploy!

In the weeks to follow, Joe David made sure that Miss Martha heard of his interest in another young girl in the valley. Oh, no! What to do? Well, it did not take Miss Martha long to decided she would write a letter to Joe David Mull. It seems she had, "a change of heart and would like very much to go out for a Sunday drive. Either the buggy or the auto would be fine!"

According to my mother, "This was a very special thing I will always remember, when I wrote my 'famous' love letter to your daddy. Now, that was not a bad thing! It settles you down." With this change of heart by Martha Jane, Joe David then had to stand before Mr. William Isaac Wimpey and his dear wife, Jane, and ask for Martha's hand in marriage. Many times daddy shared with us this moment and how he contemplated different ways to approach grandpa and grandma Wimpey.

Well, finally daddy made up his mind just how he would address the issue. He called on Miss Martha one evening and sat on the porch swing with her for a little while. Before he realized it, darkness had fallen and grandpa and grandma had retired for the evening.

Knocking softly on their door, Joe and Martha walked right into their bedroom and he posed the question. "May I have Martha's hand in marriage?" Suddenly he heard loud giggles coming from the stairway passage. Daddy thought," I will find out about that later!" He listened carefully to what grandpa and grandma were saying. It seemed they both approved. Grandpa declared, "You both are old enough to know what you are doing!"

Thus, my mother's teenage years ended with her marriage in 1927. In her words, "I turned 20 in April, and Joe had turned 27, on February 18, 1927. We were married for 65 years. You don't hear about such marriages these days!"

Ilustration 4. Wedding Ceremony at T. C. Moore's residence.

My mother and father were married at the residence of the Justice of Peace, Mr. Thomas Covington Moore, in the vicinity of the Moss Church on Tusquittee, February 20, 1927. For the ceremony, my mother wore a light blue, wool dress. My father wore a three piece, light grey, wool suit.

Now, back to those giggles heard during Joe's most nervous moment, standing before his future father-in-law, while asking for Martha's hand in marriage. Who could that have been, enjoying the moment? Well, it was none other than Martha's youngest brother, George Aaron Wimpey!

It seems this young fellow, who was only eleven years old at the time, had been listening to all the conversations of that special evening. The approval that Joe David had received from his future mother-in-law and father-in-law must have pleased the young George immensely.

All daddy's life, Uncle George remained close to him. In daddy's final days on this earth, Uncle George visited him every day at the hospital; making daddy cheerful as they recalled so many precious memories. Ironically, on the very day of my daddy's passing - just moments afterwards; Uncle George came walking down the hospital corridor for his daily visit. My mother greeted him by saying, "George, Joe is gone!"

Chapter 3

From the Slagel Place to the Herbert Place

After my parents were married on February 20, 1927, they spent their honeymoon moving into a house close to grandma Mull. Their rental home was called the 'Slagel Place' on lower Tusquittee. It was a two-room cabin with a porch. Nearby, the Tusquittee Creek flowed swiftly out of the mountains. Mama and daddy were able to farm and grow a garden. Daddy worked as a farmer or a 'sharecropper' whereby he was able to farm more land. His father, Calvin Monroe, was mighty good to help Joe with the planting of corn and farming the land.

Daddy began in the early spring, hauling out manure from the barn. This he would spread over the potato patch and roasting-ear corn patch. Trading eggs or other goods; he would soon be able to get seed potatoes and vegetable seeds for the garden. About once each year Calvin and Joe would make the long wagon-train journey down to Murphy to obtain needed farm supplies. On this trip there would be many folks making the haul to and from Murphy. It would require camping overnight by the Hiawassee River just outside Murphy. Then they would return to Tusquittee the following day. When daddy would tell us of this adventure, it seems that he enjoyed such a tough challenge.

In March, he would plant the Irish potatoes along with some English peas. When April brought warmer weather, the second plowing and spreading of manure would be done. It is easy to imagine how mama would gather the hen eggs and 'set the hens' for a new brood of baby chicks.

With good crops in the fields, they were able to feed themselves and their farm animals. Daddy was a good farmer. From Calvin he had learned the ways of trapping wild game. Of course, grandma Mull and granny Wimpey were always willing to help out whenever extra things were needed.

On May 3, 1928, their first child, William Monroe Mull, was born at the Slagel Place. He was named in honor of both his grandfathers. In later years, I remember my daddy saying, "William was a pretty baby!" Daddy often expressed much love for his first-born child.

The following year, on December 1, 1929, their first daughter was born. She was named in honor of her grandmothers. Ida Jane was also described as 'a pretty baby' but she had dark hair and dark brown eyes, unlike her blond, blue-eyed brother, William Monroe.

It was a cold, dark winter in 1929. In the little cabin, with only a fireplace and small cook stove, staying warm was a challenge every morning, noon and night! Keeping a warm fire burning; preparing meals; while taking care of two babies was work a plenty for my mother.

Illustration 5. William Monroe and Ida Jane Mull, 1930.

Daddy was struggling to find 'extra' work and was well aware of how things seem to be going downhill for them. When the news got around to them that THE DEPRESSION of 1930 had set in, daddy wondered, "When will it end?"

As 1931 rolled around and mama was expecting their third child, they were able to move to a larger farm, called the Herbert Place. There they rented the small house from Tom and Edna Herbert. The house was close to the railroad tracks and about two miles from Hayesville.

This became the birthplace for their second son, John, named in honor of two uncles; their second daughter, Eddie Lee, named in honor of two aunts; and their fifth child. The first four children had been strong babies with no complications when they were born. However, this was not the case for their fifth child.

Dr. J. M. Sullivan assisted in mama's delivery but was unable to get the newborn to start breathing. As the baby began turning blue, the doctor was losing hope for the baby. Daddy was standing very close and heard the doctor whisper a frightening prognosis. Quickly stepping out into the warm night; daddy looked up into the starry sky. With his eyes filled with tears he prayed, "Please, Dear Lord, don't let our new baby girl die!"

Going back into the cabin and approaching mama's bedside; daddy heard a wee gasp from the newborn. Dr. Sullivan nodded his head and gave daddy a reassuring smile. The baby was going to make it! She was named Bennie Louise, in honor of her two aunts, Bennie Lee Wimpey and Lou Mull.

It was not easy for baby Bennie Louise or the family as the weeks passed into months. Ida Jane recalls how anxious they all were about Bennie's condition. Often she still had difficulty with her breathing. Of course mama had to get back to her house work, gardening and preparing food for winter. As she would get ready to go to the garden, mama would tell Jane, "Watch the baby. Make sure she doesn't stop breathing!"

At the Herbert Place early childhood events were being experienced by William and Ida Jane. One such fond memory was that of watching and listening for the 'Peavine' train to come into the depot. Conductor

Charlie would pull down on the cord and wave to the children as the train rolled into town. Daddy had told the two youngsters that Mr. Charlie was their special friend. Often times at 10:00 a.m. they would wait upon the hill to watch the train rolling into the station. Sometimes they would be joined by their Uncle Johnny, who might be playing at their house. They all found 'waiting for the train' an exciting event in their day. The train may have been bringing in fertilizer and feed grain or taking out tan bark and acid wood; but for the children, the 'Peavine Special' was bringing Charlie's cheerful greeting and exciting train whistle just for them! It was great fun just to imagine how it would be to travel without a horse and wagon.

Photo 9. 'Peavine' train coming into the Depot, circa 1934.
(Courtesy of Bob Cunningham, 2006.)

Starting school at age five and six was a great experience for Jane and William, in 1934. They were both enrolled in the first grade and rode the bus to school in Hayesville, just 'two miles' away. Jane remembers that she and her brother enjoyed learning and made good grades in school.

By the time they were in the third grade they had grown accustomed to riding the bus and getting along well. But one cold winter day as they stood waiting on the bus, they realized they had missed the bus. Rather than going back home and missing a day of school, they decided it would be best if they walked to school. That was not a bad idea as it was only two miles to school.

However, as they walked along, the cold, winter weather got worse. The sleet started coming down on their tiny bodies dressed too lightly. Finally, when they arrived at school they appeared to be frozen blue. Jane recalls, "We were shivering so, our teeth were chattering. Dear Ms. Mabel Thompson wrapped us in her overcoat and seated us beside the radiator. It took us most of the day to thaw out. I will never forget that day and the goodness of that kind teacher!"

Another childhood story which William relates with great clarity, deals with Ida Jane getting a new sweater and cap; which in itself was a miracle in those days! While at school, Jane had allowed a little girl friend to wear either the sweater or cap or both.

Upon arriving home, William promptly told his mother, "Ida Jane let a little girl wear her cap and sweater today at school!" Of course Jane responded, "I did not!" Well, this did not set well with my mama. When she could not get 'the truth' she quickly marched them behind the house. They knew what was going to happen. Suddenly, they got their story straight!

Chores the children were expected to carry out each day included carrying water from a mountain spring; carrying in stove wood and fire wood; gathering the eggs; feeding the cattle and many other necessary duties. With successful crops in the fields, a good milk cow, a few laying hens and the garden vegetables, the family was able to get by during the depression years. These years seemed to linger on for the family.

My mother would secretly wish that she and Joe could find a place of their own. She was weary with renting a small place and working so hard just to get by from one season to the next. It was evident to the children that their parents held a strong faith in God and relied on prayers to bring them through adverse times. Surely, with hard work and faith in the Lord, they would find a way.

One day when daddy came home and told mama he thought he had found a place he might buy, she was so happy! He told her the house was rough and not finished. But it was situated on about six acres of land with a mountain spring and a branch for the cattle. With great assertiveness, mama replied, "I don't care! Just go buy it!"

Well, that request was easier said than done. Daddy had to figure a way he could trade stock for the place, because he sure did not have any cash. It only took him a few days till he came up with stock sufficient to trade with Mr. Jim Long, who owned the land in the Matheson Cove.

Trading one good horse, a milk cow, a hog and $100.00; daddy was finally able to get their very own place in the Cove. Mama had not even seen the place but she assured daddy it would be just fine. Thus, Joe and Martha bid the Herbert Place 'adieu.' It was the dead of winter in 1936, when they made their move to the Matheson Cove. The house may not have been fine but mama loved that little house till the day she died.

Chapter 4

Settling into the Cove

In the winter of 1936, Joe and Martha Mull made their fateful move into the Matheson Cove. While at the Herbert Place, three of their children had been born. John, the second son, was born on July 3, 1931, and named in honor of daddy's Uncle John. Their second daughter, Eddie Lee, was born on November 3, 1932, and named in honor of mama's twin sisters. Their third daughter, Bennie Louise, born on July 5, 1934, was now a healthy two and a half year old.

On a cold winter day, mama and daddy loaded their few belongings into their wagon and moved into the Cove. The three younger children were watched by Aunt Ella Vee Wimpey during moving day. As they rode along a small dirt trail leading back to their farm, mama saw the little house nestled in a thick forest of pine trees. Through her eyes, it looked like a good place to live!

Walking up to the front door made of rough planks; she quickly realized they had a problem. There was not a doorknob! Examining the door closely she discovered a wooden latch attached to a string. The door had to be opened from the INSIDE!

Daddy began searching for an opening as he walked around the house. He found a small window at the back of the house. But it was much too small to enter. Turning to his daughter, Bennie Louise, he said, "We'll send you inside to open the door." She was gently placed in the opening. Slowly she walked into the strange house.

Today, Bennie recalls, "I can still remember walking into this real big room. As I looked up, I could see daylight coming through the cracks at the top of the house. I tiptoed over to the latched door and pulled the string. Like magic, the door swung open!" Thus, the family entered their new house. Finally, my mother was able to enjoy her own place in which she could raise her family. Somehow, it seemed just fine!

Even before the move Ida Jane had talked with daddy about her anxiety regarding finding the new place, when she and William got off the school bus. It was a long walk from the Tom Mason place, where all the children coming into the Cove were let off the bus. Daddy assured Jane there would be lots of children walking around the Matheson Cove road to their homes. One of those children would show her the way to her new home.

However, that very first day seemed mighty scary to William and Jane. The forest was dense around the new home place. They did not know the strange children. As they all walked along one of the teenage girls, Reba Ledford, spoke to Ida Jane. Reba assured her, "You will not get lost. I will show you exactly which wooded path to take to your new home."

Reba made them feel better on their first arrival to their new home. Suddenly, the many children walking along with them did not seem so strange. Jane was very glad that Reba had talked with them.

Entering their new home, William and Jane looked about and saw things were set up and everything appeared to be in place. Yet they knew there were many tasks to be done and their parents could always use their help with the younger children.

Later on, after the evening prayers, Jane learned from her father that Reba lived on the farm next to her new home place. Reba also had lots of brothers and sisters. William and Jane did not know that in Mr. and Mrs. Bob Ledford's family there was a son and a daughter who would soon become their dear friends.

In later years, Bennie Louise related, "Daddy soon had our roof fixed and the cracks filled." A small spring which flowed out of the ground near the house was quickly surrounded by a *Spring House.* It was here that the family was able to get their fresh water until the well was dug. Also, the milk and butter were kept cool in the spring house. It would be a long time before electricity would come to the Cove.

My grandfather Wimpey helped daddy dig the well on our home place. They very cleverly dug the well so that the well curbing was on the back porch. There was a windlass, rope and bucket to draw the water. The water was pulled up slowly, one bucket at a time. The children were often reminded, "Don't waste the water!"

When there was a severe draught the well would go dry. Then daddy would have to sink the well. He had learned from granddad Wimpey, the skills required to dig a well. The well was mighty nice, being enclosed and near the kitchen and cook stove. Mama said, "We felt lucky, as most folks did not have a good well. They had to carry their water from a mountain spring or from a good neighbor's well."

There was lots of new ground to be cleared and prepared for planting in the spring of 1937. Hard work was just a way of life in the family. On a daily basis, our parents ask God's blessing and protection from all harm. Before each meal, as well as morning and evening, my parents would conduct their devotionals to God. Approaching the birth of her sixth child; mama prayed to God the child would be healthy; recalling the difficulties at the birth of her beautiful daughter, Bennie Louise.

And so it was, the fourth daughter was born on March 16, 1937. She was named Mary Jo, in honor of our Aunt Mary Mease and daddy. Bennie Louise was happy to have a new little sister, but for some reason she really wanted to remain the baby. But Eddie Lee helped Bennie adjust and learn to enjoy their new sister.

Mama's sister, Ella Vee, always came to stay with the family, when a new baby was born. That March, she again helped with the many meals, washings and house cleaning. Everyone was looking forward to spring and warm weather. Then they would not have to worry so much about gathering firewood and trying to stay warm.

Soon spring arrived and mama was able to be outside and help with all the planting and gardening. She and my father worked side by side to make the new farm become their very own special place. Times had been hard during the early depression years and seemed to persist throughout the 1930's.

According to Bennie Louise, "Looking back to earlier years, when my father had been a 'sharecropper' we could see that things were changing for the better. We made our own music, sang praises to God, and tried to love one another. We were certainly not afraid of hard work. We always had hope of better times in those early years!"

Part 2
Dazzling Progress

Chapter 5

Second Half Coming Up

After my parents and their five children had moved into the Matheson Cove, in the winter of 1936, they seemed to be off to a good start. They had more room in the new house and my father, along with help from my granddad Wimpey, had been able to winterize the house. William and John were growing into strong young fellows and were able to help with all the farming and clearing of the new ground.

Photo 10. John, Bill with 'Ole Bob' and 'Ted,' circa, 1938.
(Courtesy of Ida Jane Rowland, 2006.)

Eddie Lee and Ida Jane were old enough to help mama with the new baby. Bennie Louise was learning more about her new sister. She enjoyed being outside where everyone was working.

As the early autumn of 1938, passed into September, the family was to suffer their greatest test of survival. Another baby was on the way and daddy was contemplating how to expand the house to make room for all the children. At about the time my mother was expecting her seventh child, 'the lucky one,' she contacted the measles and was very ill.

On September 9, 1938, I was born and my mother named me Eva Nell, in honor of her dear neighbor, Mrs. Eva Gibson. Her illness went through every member of the family. Even my father was very ill. The family was quarantined. My sister, Bennie, recalls, "It was really bad with everyone so sick with high fevers. We were in bed and unable to do anything for ourselves. Mrs. Claudia Passmore, a mid-wife, and Miss Reba Ledford came to help us. If it had not been for our good neighbors, I don't know what we would have done!"

Flashing forward to 2005, that same Reba Ledford, only sixteen years old that fateful time in September, came back into my life in Oak Ridge, Tennessee. That summer day my phone rang and the caller said, "I am trying to find Eva Nell Mull and I don't know if I have the right number." Quickly, I assured the 'unknown' caller she did indeed have the correct telephone number. I knew by the way she talked she was surely from the Cove. I listened carefully as she told me, "I am Reba Ledford from the Matheson Cove. When I was a young girl, I remember setting up all night with your mama when she was so ill. She had a brand new baby. There was another lady there and we sat up all night. We were so afraid both Mrs. Mull and her new baby were going to die!"

By that point in the phone conversation, my composure was slipping fast. I did not know what to say to this lady, whom, as far as I knew, I had never seen in my whole life. "What year were you with my mother and the new baby?" I asked. She replied, "Oh, I don't remember. But I do know I was sixteen years old." Then I did the math and asked, "Are you 83 years old now?" Reba responded, "Yes, I am! How did you know?" By that time I was fighting back the tears but was able to say in a shaky voice, "I was that new baby!" She was just about as surprised as I that she had found that new baby, way over in Tennessee, sixty-seven years later.

In our conversation, Reba explained how she had left the Cove, after graduation. She had boarded a bus in Murphy, NC, and bid the Matheson Cove 'goodbye!' Where did this beautiful girl go? Ironically, she went to Oak Ridge, TN. There Reba worked for several years.

Photo 11. Reba Ledford, at K-25, U-235 Enrichment Plant, 1943.
(Courtesy of Reba Ledford Rigsbee, 2006.)

You could say that Reba and I have a lot in common. I invited Reba for a visit to my house and gardens in Oak Ridge. She readily accepted and in a few days she arrived. When I answered the door and looked into her face, it was like looking into her mother's kind face. Listening to her speak was like hearing Mrs. Ledford talk. All I could say was, "You are just like your mother!" For a moment I was back in the Cove. Her smile and laughter made me realize I was indeed the 'lucky one' of the Mull children!

Back in the Cove during 1938, there was talk about terrible battles being fought in other parts of the world. It was not easy to get much news up in the Cove. According to my folks, we had no electricity and we sure did not have a battery powered radio. My father would go to the 'Square' and talk with the other men of the community about what might be going on in Europe or some other faraway place. For certain, we were very isolated from the outside world.

We were isolated with the exception of one household item, which most folks did not have in their home. We had a TELEPHONE. Yes sir! We had a big box hanging on the wall. We had a phone on which you could pick up the receiver, turn a little crank and hear Aunt Lizzie say "Central!" Blind Jim Penland had brought the switchboard up to Hayesville, in 1916, from Atlanta, and installed it in town.

Photo 12. Switchboard and Blind Jim Penland, 1940.
(Courtesy of James S. Wike, 2006.)

Daddy ran a wire from our house, through the woods, over the Cherry Knob and on down the Cherry Mountain to Hayesville. Any time there was icy weather; which tore down the trees or poles on which he had strung the wire; he would go out and fix the break. Daddy had us talking on the phone; everyone except Mary Jo and me! The two of us seemed to speak a foreign language – all our own!

In the autumn of 1940, everyone was getting nervous about bits of news that was getting through to us in the Cove. I had just turned two years old and was getting worse by the day with my enunciation. My older sisters found it very amusing to try and figure out just what Mary Jo and I were saying in our 'foreign' language. A few years ago, when the movie "Nell" was released, the actress, Jody Foster, really go into my head about such strange ways of talking in early childhood.

As the autumn turned to winter in the Cove, the time was coming when mama would give birth to her eighth baby. Would she have another daughter? The family would have to just wait and see if she might have a son. Well, indeed she did! On November 6, 1940, my mother had a new baby boy. She chose to name him James Carl Mull. The name was again in honor of someone very special. That person was our Uncle Carl Christian Jensen, who had come over from Denmark, in 1929. He worked at Coble Creamery, down on Brasstown and daddy said he would give us ice cream anytime we wanted it. We all loved Uncle Carl!

When Uncle Carl learned of Martha's new son, whom she had named after him, he was delighted. It was only a few weeks later when the biggest crate we had ever seen was delivered to our house. Inside was a Victrola shipped from some faraway place by our dear Uncle Carl, who was serving in the United States Army. The Victrola was to be our new baby brother's gift. We were plum proud of the baby and his gift! We all gathered round that fancy Victrola, taking turns, winding it up with a crank. It was our only source for listening to music. It seemed mighty special; sitting by the fireside on a cold, winter night and being able to listen to those wonderful tunes recorded on the big thick records.

Photo 13. Uncle Carl's gift to James Carl Mull, 1940.
(Courtesy of James Carl Mull, 2006.)

A few years ago, Uncle Carl's daughter, Jane Jensen, was writing a documentary about her father. She shared with James a 'Certificate of Apprenticeship,' which had enabled Uncle Carl to get a job in America. She shared his diary with James; wherein he revealed his love for our Aunt Bennie and just how much he missed his family over in Denmark.

Being born only two years apart, James Carl and I kind of grew up together on our isolated farm. Our pre-school days were spent chasing roosters down and then watching mama chop off their heads. We became clever about 'staying out of trouble!' However, once in a while we had to take a quick detour to stay in the clear.

One such time occurred just after our baby sister, Nancy Sue, was born on April 27, 1942. Our Aunt Ella Vee had grown weary with all the racket James and I were making in the front room. She grabbed a broom and before we knew it, she had whacked us both on the behinds.

Out the front door we dashed and hit the ground running, as we leaped from the front porch. We ran like a 'mad dog' was after us; running hard all the way to the edge of the pine thicket. Finding a log on which to sit; we mulled over Aunt Ella Vee's whacking and decided that from now on, we better walk softly around her.

As summer time came on, James and I continued our outdoor chores. We enjoyed the warmer weather and trying to catch crawfish in the branch using a toe sack. We were good at chasing chickens, hunting rabbits or 'making hats' out of big popular leaves.

However, one day things really hit bottom! I had climbed the wooden fence encircling the pig lot. I leaned a little too far trying to reach a choice leaf that would have made a fine hat. WHAM! I fell into the pig pen! What an uproar I made as I screamed, "Go get mama!" James's brown eyes were so big! I thought he had seen a ghost when he looked at me. He ran so fast he left dust devils spinning in the lane!

Illustration 6. James leaving dust devils in the lane, 1943.

Mama had already heard my woeful screams and soon appeared. She was praying softly through her apron, which partially covered her astonished face. Imagine one chubby child covered in hog 'mud' with her right arm hanging at a strange angle. Mama knew I was in deep! Somehow, I was able to crawl on my knees and one good arm to the edge of the pen. She helped me roll under the fence and move painfully toward the house.

In addition to thinking my arm was going to fall off from the pain, I was thinking, "Today is not Saturday. We only get baths on Saturday!" But, it did not take mama long to get me cleaned up and wrapped in a blanket. She helped me to her bed, saying, "Now, lay real still till your daddy gets home."

That waiting seemed to be the longest day of my summer. Daddy finally came home from digging a well and was so tired. I was only five years old, but I knew how hard my daddy had to work just to make a dollar. As he shook his head slowly, he told mama, "We will be back as soon as we can. I must get Eva Nell to the hospital. We have to get her arm set!"

He gently put me on his back. As we headed down through the pasture on foot, I was sure we would never make it to Murphy. When he got on the foot log, crossing the branch, I held on a little tighter. He laughed and assured me we would not fall again!

Out on the highway, we stopped at our neighbors. Daddy asked Mr. Roy Gibson if he would please drive us to the hospital in Murphy. Mr. Gibson did so but he did not wait for us to get my arm set. That took a long time and then daddy placed me on his back to begin our twenty mile hike back home.

It seemed like ages before someone stopped and gave us a ride. We were not the finest looking pair; daddy slowly carrying me down the road! Finally a man stopped and told us to get in the back of his truck. Daddy kind of hesitated when he saw a horse tied in the bed of the truck. Then he placed me very carefully in the bed of the truck and settled in beside me, with a sigh of relief. He was so tired.

It did not take long for the horse to start acting up and it really scared daddy. He managed to move to the cab of the truck and rap on it with his fist. The man stopped the truck; cursing and yelling at us; he screamed, "What do you want?" My daddy spoke of his fear that the horse might kick his little girl. The driver's response was NOT polite!

Illustration 7: Ride home from the hospital, 1943.

We huddled close together as far as we could manage from the horse's hoofs. I could hear daddy softly praying for the Lord to protect us. The man drove on toward the Cove, letting us off at the main road. Then as night was falling, my daddy had to make that long walk across the fields. In the dusk of the summer evening, he carefully stepped along the foot log and hurried up the bluff to the house, still carrying me. Mama was so relieved when we finally got home safely.

Turning six years old in September, I was now ready for the first grade. Well, nobody knew just how unprepared I really was for the first grade. My oldest sister, Ida Jane, kind of knew. From her surrogate mother role, she knew I could not speak plainly enough to 'make sense' at school.

On the first day of school, Jane held my hand as we walked from the school bus down to the wooden building, which housed the first grade. By the grip of her hand, her gentle reassuring words and my pounding heart, I knew I was in deep, again!

During the first few days of school, I never spoke a word. I was afraid someone would hear me and start laughing at the way I talked. Then they would be in trouble for laughing at me. Then I would be in trouble for teaching them a lesson or two. Finally, if the word got home to my mama and daddy, there would be more trouble for me when I got home.

The first grade teacher, Miss Moses, kind of scared me with her unsmiling face. I tried very hard to avoid her wrath which she could quickly rain down on any naughty child. But, alas, it soon happened on a warm, October afternoon. We were all lined up 'straight' to march back into our classroom. As Miss Moses turned to lead us inside, I dashed to the water fountain to get one final drink. I thought, "I can be back before she can say 'scat'!" Well, it was amazing how quickly she could say 'scat' and even more quickly snatch her paddle from the desk. Fortunately, neither Ida Jane nor the other children informed mama of my 'encounter' with the paddle.

It was always great to get off the bus, which now came into the Cove. The driver, Mr. Wayne Long, would drop us at the end of our lane. Many of the pine trees had been cleared and we could see mama standing on the porch, waiting for her children to come running home.

The mouth watering smell of freshly-baked sweet taters in the big old black pan was waiting for us. Them sweet taters covered in a little blackstrap molasses made a fine afternoon snack! Then we would have to get to our chores straight away. Darkness would fall sometimes before daddy would get home from his well-digging job.

My daddy often said he became interested in digging wells for other people because of his experiences with granddad Wimpey, back when they dug our well in 1937. He did not put much confidence in the method of using a divining rod to determine exactly where to start digging for a well.

There was one fellow, Mr. Earl Crawford, who was supposed to be able to find the 'right' spot to dig a well. Using a forked willow branch; holding the two ends firmly in his hands with the third pointing straight ahead; Earl would walk about searching for water. The spot where the pointing end rotated up or down was where the water would be found. This method was called 'Willow Witching.' Daddy preferred to just use common sense instead of divination.

Digging wells back then was 'a dangerous business' and required great strength. But anytime daddy learned of a neighbor or friend who needed a well dug on their farm, he would accept the challenge. He was almost apologetic when he would tell the folks; "I have to be paid a dollar a foot to dig your well." Then he would quickly add, "If that is 'easy' digging! If I hit rock it will run more!" The folks understood that with rock, daddy would have to use dynamite to break the stone.

But sometimes folks were down and out. They would ask daddy to dig their well but then could not pay him what they owed. He would have to come home in damp and muddy clothes. Then he would have to share his hard day of disappointment. Sitting by the fire; trying to get warm; he would have to tell mama he had not been paid for his digging. Those times were dismal and sad, especially when mama would cry.

But most of the time, when folks came by our house or sent word to daddy, he would load up his gear and head out. As I remember, my brother, James Carl, was often helping daddy in those days. James recalls, "I always enjoyed the first day of digging! Daddy would throw out the dirt as he dug down to about ten feet before he would have to set up the windlass, rope and bucket. As daddy would throw out the dirt, I would load the dirt into a wheelbarrow and take it nearby to spread it thinly on the ground."

The well had to be dug precisely with a three foot diameter. Daddy always said, "The walls have to be very straight as tile may have to be lowered into the well to prevent the dirt from caving!"

On the second day of digging, the windlass was set in place. A 'modified' thirty gallon barrel was used to haul the dirt up to the top. There were no OSHA regulations back then, but daddy would put on his hard hat; put one leg in the cut-off barrel; and as he would say, "ease down" into the well using his free foot to guide him along the wall.

In the earlier years, John and William would work the windlass as daddy would dig the wells. Later on, James would be on one side of the windlass and sometimes I would be on the other side of the windlass; lowering our daddy down into the well.

Using a short handle mattock and spade, daddy would dig and very precisely shape the sides of the well. The dirt was pulled from the bottom one barrel at a time. Slowly and with great effort, daddy would repeat the process, day by day, until he would hit a vein of water.

According to James, "It was a happy day when the dirt turned to mud. Of course that would make the hauling more difficult but we knew it would be only four or five more feet of digging. Daddy knew when he had hit a good supply of water! Then the well was finished and the depth of the water was determined by where the water was first struck."

When the well had to be 'tiled' daddy would call on granddad Wimpey to furnish him with the tile. Granddad was able to make the tile right in his workshop. He was a great craftsman and a good mentor for daddy in the early years.

The number of wells daddy dug in the county is unknown. I was surprised to recently discover a couple of wells that are declared to be 'mighty good wells,' which he had dug. According to my brother, David, there are several wells daddy dug which are still being used today.

Photo 14. One of the many *Wells* my daddy dug, circa, 1950.
(Courtesy of Carl Moore, 2006.)

Of course there were times when dynamite had to be used to break up the rock. A hand-cranked air pump was used to pull the fumes from the well, after blasting had occurred. This pump could be reversed to pump fresh air into the well.

I can remember how worried mama would be on the days she knew daddy would be 'shooting dynamite.' He would come home so tired and complaining of an 'ole dynamite headache' at the supper table. I always felt sorry for my daddy having to work so hard for a dollar.

It would be fair to say my daddy was a 'trusting soul' as he put his life on the line to dig a well for folks. There were a couple of bad accidents that almost took him away from us. One time a barrel of dirt actually fell on daddy. Thank goodness he had on his hard hat; as that was all that saved him. Another time he went down into a well before the fumes had been completely cleared. It was just a miracle that daddy survived that accident!

That particular well belonged to Mr. Wayne Moore upon Tidwell Hill, on Tusquittee. Actually, it was an existing well which daddy had been asked to sink. According to Mr. Moore's son, Tommy Moore, the well was 85 feet deep and every winter it would go dry. The well had been tiled and provided mighty good water for the folks. That was why Mr. Moore wanted to keep the well, instead of digging another well.

Tommy was just a little fellow back in 1947, on the day daddy collapsed and almost died. But today Tommy recalls, "I've heard the story so many times, I think I remember every detail! My daddy would not let Joe go back down in the well. After they hauled Joe out and helped him revive from the fumes, my daddy said, 'Joe, you have a family to care for! There is no way I will let you go back down in that well today!'"

Fortunately, daddy fully recovered from the accident. It was not long until he quit the well-digging business. He left us and went up north, to Canton, Ohio. Much like in his younger days, daddy was able to find employment in the steel mills.

Wages in the steel mills were much higher than in well-digging. But mama would not hear to our leaving the Cove and going up north to live. Her heartfelt belief was that we all belonged together, in the Cove!

Chapter 6

Horse-drawn Wagons and Faraway Places

Riding to church in a horse-drawn wagon had been going on in my family for a long time. I never thought that someday this would end. Attending church and behaving properly was a lesson a child could learn very quickly. It was understandable to me that daddy did not tolerate 'foolishness' in his children, or for that matter anyone. The children in our family learned this fact at an early age.

We made our journey back and forth to church services three times a week, rain or shine. Mama and daddy would sit on the seat of the wagon. The children would get into the back of the wagon. In the wintertime we would wrap up in quilts my mama and grandma Wimpey had quilted. Often we would pick up folks who were walking to church. Sometimes neighbors would simply wait until we came by their house and just come out to 'get on board' for a ride to church.

Our horses were very gentle and if handled properly there was never a problem. But one fine Sunday morning Mary Jo and Bennie Louise climbed in the wagon as soon as church service was finished. I had barely gotten into the wagon when, all of a sudden, the horses bolted away like wild stallions.

As I looked back toward the church, there was daddy standing in the church yard with a horrified look on his face. We were screaming our heads off and going at break-neck speed toward the main road. Across the highway we went, bouncing along toward the graveyard! As we approached the cemetery we had all stopped screaming. My sisters might have been praying silently. But I was watching those tombstones coming at us as we climbed the hill. We went right into the United Methodist Cemetery! Just as we were about to crash into the gravesites, the horses stopped. It must have been a miracle! I looked back and saw daddy running toward us and mama standing in the church yard praying. I thought, "It ain't going to be good for whichever sister undid them reins!" As far as daddy was concerned, scaring horses was a lot worse than showing your ignorance! We were in big trouble!

Illustration 8: Run Away Horses! 1943.

Daddy came up through the Cemetery to retrieve the team of horses and the wagon. My sisters and I sat motionless and 'real quiet' like in the wagon. No one spoke a word! Daddy got in and drove us back to the church; got out of the wagon; tied the reins and helped mama into her seat. I was still shaking as everybody else got into the wagon and we rode away in silence. Another miracle!

As a child listening to the sermons in the Church of God, I was easily scared. The Book of Revelations, with the Hellfire and Brimstone portions, was particularly disturbing to me. But what really set my heart to pounding was when a 'strange' preacher man would bring rattle snakes in a box to church. It was plum scary, especially so, when their rattles got to sounding off.

The preacher was generally a traveling minister from Tennessee. His stay always seemed to be kind of brief. Maybe it was brief cause folks could make up their minds, real quick like, as to whether or not they were going to participate in the 'snake handling' portion of the services. It sure did not take my daddy long to make up his mind. You may recall my daddy did not tolerate 'foolishness' under any circumstance.

In my younger years I did not know just how instrumental my mother and father had been in the establishment of the Church of God on Fort Hembree Road. I suppose it all began back when daddy was a tiny boy living on Tusquittee. In later years, daddy recalled how he and his young friend were playing one day near his house when a finely dressed lady stopped to say hello. She informed the boys, "You young fellows should be in Sunday School!" Daddy was surprised to learn about 'Sunday School' and that he needed to be there. Soon he went home and asked his mother if he could go to Sunday school the next Sunday. Further, he inquired, "What do I do in Sunday School?" His mama consented, "Yes, you can go. All you do is just go in, take a seat, and be real quiet!"

Thus began his many years of devotion and support for the Church of God. Times were different in the early days. Tolerance for the church was sometimes difficult to achieve. For a long time, there was harsh resentment toward building a Church of God on Tusquittee. Three times the church buildings were burned to the ground by folks who did not want a church to be built in their community.

Way back in the early 1930's, before there was a Church of God in Hayesville, folks in the Cove would gather on Wednesday night to have a prayer service at our home. A good neighbor, Mr. Charlie Hampton, was very faithful to bring his Bible and visit for prayer service on Wednesday evenings after supper. Of course he was not our uncle, but all the children called him Uncle Charlie. My older brothers and sisters still remember Uncle Charlie with great fondness.

One cold and snowy day in January, 1938, the school children were walking from the bus stop toward home around the Cove road. Suddenly they saw a man laying beside the road all covered in snow. There was a newspaper covering his face. Ida Jane recalls, "We saw it was Uncle Charlie Hampton. It seemed so terrible to see Uncle Charlie lying there in the snow! We took off running like our heads were on fire; me going home to get daddy; William going to get Mr. Tom Mason. I thought, 'If I run fast enough, maybe we can save Uncle Charlie!' Seeing Uncle Charlie all covered in snow that day is something I will never forget!"

Daddy and Mr. Tom carried Uncle Charlie a short distance to his little cabin and laid him near the hearth. After building a fire in the fireplace; once more daddy turned to examine Uncle Charlie. Daddy said, "He struggled slightly and then he was gone." Uncle Charlie Hampton (b. 10-17-1863; d. 1-13-1938) left his family and the good folks in the Cove, that cold winter day, but he will not be forgotten!

Everyone in the community was saddened by Uncle Charlie's passing away. He had been one of the earliest settlers in the Matheson Cove. It would not be the same without him. However, mama and daddy did not give up on their prayer meetings. The harsh reality of church burnings on Tusquittee did not discourage them. Daddy was able to glean building materials from an old building which was being torn down. He and other devoted members of the Church of God started building a small structure on the site of the present day church, located on Fort Hembree Road.

As the years passed, daddy and mama helped other groups of good people establish churches in their own communities. Folks called such an effort of coming together, 'Brush Arbor Day.' The men folks would build a simple arbor out of small trees and brush for covering the structure. They would place split logs inside the arbor to serve as pews.

The women folks would plan for an ALL DAY singing and dinner on the ground. This would be kind of a 'camp meeting' in the summer time, with preaching and singing for a week or so. The closing event; all day singing and dinner on the ground; would provide an opportunity for everyone to enjoy the fellowship. Hopefully, this effort would attract other good folks to the services and they might choose to become members of the new church. There were many communities in which daddy and mama helped establish a new Church of God.

In October, 1967, daddy and mama participated in a 'Re-enactment' of Brush Arbor Day up on Tusquittee. Other participants who were charter members of the Church of God included Mrs. Dora Nelson, Mrs. Dora Davenport, Mrs. Iova Patterson, Mrs. Bertha Blankenship, Mr. Zeb Johnson, and Mr. Emerson Davenport.

During daddy's presentation that special day, to an audience of about 250 people, he stated: "I became interested in the Church of God as early as 1908, while attending a Pentecostal revival conducted by the Reverend C. R. Curtis. This was on Tusquittee, where the church had been burned by critics. The revival was being conducted in the Episcopal Church. The critics did not like the revival being held there, so they burned that church!"

In the following photo of the 'Re-enactment' some of the participants include the driver, Mr. C. D. Ledford, a friend of the church; Mrs.

Dora Nelson and her daughter, Mrs. Ottie Faye Nelson Ashe; and daddy, to the far right in the photograph.

Photo 15. 'Re-enactment' of Brush Arbor Day, October, 1967.
(Courtesy of Mrs. Ottie Fay Nelson Ashe, 2006.)

In the early 1940's we had heard talk about electricity coming to the Cove. But it seemed the break out of World War II somehow put a stop to that progress. This was due to all the men folks being called off to the war. There were no raw materials available to build the power stations and lines. Soon our brother, William, along with our cousins Ray and Paul Mease, as well as our neighbor boys would all go off to war.

The use of oil lamps for studying our lessons at the kitchen table would continue, just like our riding to church in the wagon. It was a simple but good way of life for us. This was especially so, when we considered what our soldier boys were going to experience in faraway places.

On our farm, great effort was required in gathering and preparing food for the winter months. Just about the whole summer long, picking berries was expected of every child big enough to carry a bucket. Often daddy would take us to the berry patches around the edge of the fields. According to Jane, "You did not stop picking until your bucket was full! If you complained that 'there's no more berries here, Papa!' daddy would come over; stomp down the weeds and show you real quick like there was plenty more berries to pick."

We depended on our canned goods, milk and eggs to pay for lunches at school. During the early forties, there were five children in school. Jane recalls, "I would take a half-gallon of green beans and trade it for five lunch tickets. Each ticket cost five cents! That sounds like a pretty good deal, but those lunches didn't amount to much food!"

One situation that happened at school, which mama and daddy never learned about, dealt with those lunch tickets. It seemed the individual tickets were printed on both sides. Plus they were fairly thick tickets. It seemed to William that if a lunch ticket was carefully torn apart a fellow would have himself *TWO* lunch tickets. This would allow him to go through the line and eat again! After all, one lunch meal was just not enough food!

When Jane learned what William and his friend were doing, she and her friend ask to join the 'double dipping' crew. According to William, "I had a good thing going till Ida Jane told her friend!" When they all wound up in Principal Ralph Smith's office, they were quaking in their homemade shoes. If mama and daddy got wind of this, they would be punished severely! Apparently, this fact was also much on the mind of the principal. Today, Jane recalls the kindness and mercy Mr. Smith exhibited toward the frightened and hungry children. All they had to do was promise never, ever to do such a thing again. You can be assured, they kept their promise!

Photo 16. *l. to r.* **Nancy Sue sitting on daddy's lap,**
James Carl, mama holding Donald Roger Mull, 1946.
(Courtesy of Ida Jane Mull Rowland, 2006.)

We younger children in the family depended on the rolling library to bring us books, as it came slowly around the Cove road. Our older siblings helped us learn to read, mainly by the lamplight. Perhaps an even more 'fulfilling' experience was the rolling store, which came by every Thursday, and stopped at the end of our lane. We could trade hen eggs or the ole hens themselves for our meager commodities. If we were lucky, the driver would toss us a piece of candy!

It was first mine and James's job to run down and catch any of the hens mama had designated to be traded. Then I would go into the hen house and gather up a dozen eggs. Ida Jane would write us a list of things we wanted to barter for and off we would go to meet the rolling store.

The driver of the rolling store had a set of scales in the back of the truck on which to hang the old hens by one leg to weigh them. Next, he would count the eggs and compute our 'bartering power.' All during that time, we did not need to say a word. All we needed to do was just give him our list. Then the driver would give us the salt, sugar, coffee or flour. Away we would go back home knowing we had done something really important that day!

Of course, during those days we had another option for purchasing our cornmeal. Mrs. Pearl McClure and her husband, Mr. Cline, had a mill for grinding corn. This required that we shell the corn and carry it in toe sacks to the mill, get it ground and give a small portion to Mrs. McClure as payment. We could also trade eggs at this store. My sister, Mary Jo and I generally had the pleasure of 'toten' the corn about a half mile to the store. But early on Mrs. Pearl had been emphatic, saying "Don't send those girls over, unless they have a note. I can't understand a word they say!"

Recently, when Jane and I visited Mrs. Pearl on her ninety-first birthday, she recalled, "Those girls had their own language! I couldn't understand a word they said. Eva Nell, I can't believe you became a teacher!" With all due respect, I quipped, "I'll bet you can't believe I even learned to speak plainly!" What precious memories!

Remembering the 'War Years' brings back sad recollections of how our cousins, Ray and Paul Mease went off to fight in the Atlantic and Pacific regions. My brother, William, was only sixteen years old, but he wanted to join the U.S. Army. Daddy would not sign for him to leave school and go off to war. But William felt strongly that he must go and was able to join and serve in Trinidad. While he was in the service he sent Eddie Lee and Ida Jane nice sweaters. He knew how much they loved pretty clothes!

One very sad time during the war, which Ida Jane vividly recalls, occurred when she was having supper with Mrs. Minnie Ledford's family. As they were all seated around the supper table; waiting for Mr. Ledford to say the blessing; Mrs. Minnie got up and went into the back room. She brought back a large picture of her son, Ralph. He was serving with General Douglas MacArthur in the Philippines. She gently placed the picture on the table. Then Mr. Ledford returned thanks and prayed to God for Ralph's safe return.

Some memories of the 'War Years' are wonderful to recall today. One is when our baby brother, Donald Roger, was born on October 5, 1945. He was a dark haired, brown eyed baby whom we adored. James recalls, "Dr. Staten assisted mama in the birth of my brother, Donald. I kept asking, 'How did the baby get here?' I was just so curious but no one would explain to me!"

Our world was simple and safe! But sad memories were being made by our soldiers in faraway places! After the war, Ralph, his brothers and William came home to the Cove. But many young soldiers did not return to their families. Ray and Paul Mease came back home bearing their war memories. Other brave men returned crippled for life.

I was only seven years old but I can recall my daddy expressing his sorrow for the tragic price some families had to pay. In early April, 1945, I remember how every teacher and every student marched from the school into Hayesville. We wanted to pay our respects to our 32nd President of the United States. Standing around the 'Square' we faced the flag flying at half-mast. Our eyes filled with tears as we sang "Home, Home On the Range" which had been President Franklin Delano Roosevelt's favorite song. Daddy thought FDR was mighty fine!

In 1947, my sister, Ida Jane, was completing her senior year at Hayesville High School. She had been deeply moved by her brother, her cousins and her dear neighbors going off to war. She had a heartfelt devotion for the cause so many young soldiers had helped defend. She felt the anguish Mrs. Ledford had known when she did not hear from Ralph for six months. She knew how mama and our Aunt Mary had worried about their sons. Jane saw the wounded returning and trying to find a way to make a living.

As graduation drew near, Jane was awarded the academic honor of addressing her fellow classmates. Her topic for her speech, which she delivered to the Class of 1947, was "World Peace." She presented it with great conviction, to every classmate and to every citizen attending the graduation ceremony. I remember very well how hard she worked in preparation for the address. Her brilliance was truly demonstrated in an extraordinary way on that graduation day!

Photo 17. Ida Jane Mull, 1947
(Courtesy of Ida Jane Mull Rowland, 2006.)

Daddy had been to the 'Square' for the latest news and came home one day, soon after Jane's graduation. I heard him tell mama, "Cline McClure told me he had never heard a finer speech!" Mama and daddy were not proud folks. But I knew in my heart that graduation day they had been proud of their daughter, Ida Jane!

Finally electricity came to the Cove! It had been more than a decade after President Roosevelt had signed the legislation for the Rural Electrification Act, on May 11, 1935. Folks up toward Shooting Creek got electricity a few years earlier, but we had to wait till after the war.

James recalls, "I will never forget the light string being pulled in our front room ceiling for the first time. The first time daddy turned on that light bulb, it was like the whole world was lighted and was something that would never be forgotten!" For me the front room seemed to be the most dazzling place in the world! We were told, 'it'll kill you!' But that electricity sure seemed nice. We no longer had to walk around with an oil lamp or study at the dimly lit kitchen table.

We were able to get rid of our old, battery powered radio. Earlier daddy had made the old radio work by running a wire to the outside and from tree to tree. The wire was run through glass tops from broken jars to get good reception. That 'technology' was gone! Now we could broaden our world of listening to all kinds of radio stations; not just WCKY in Cincinnati, Ohio! Our evening reception on WJJD, out of Chicago, Illinois, came in loud and clear! "The Mid-Day Merry Go Round" on WNOX, out of Knoxville, Tennessee, would become our 'favorite' station at dinner time. Of course the "Grand Ole Opry" on WSM out of Nashville, was our only Saturday night entertainment.

My sisters and I would listen to those sad songs and each of us would write down a portion of the lyrics. Pretty soon we would have every word memorized. Of course all my sisters could sing real well. Sadly, the same was not true for me. But if my sister, Eddie Lee, played the guitar loud enough nobody could here me anyway. So that was alright.

Along about 1948, daddy had to leave us. He went to Canton, Ohio, to find work in the steel mills; just like he had done as a young man in the 1920's. We did not want to see him go! But mama said, "He either goes to get work or we will starve to death!" That statement kind of settled our worries and stopped our tears.

We worked hard that winter, getting firewood from the Cross-tie Holler; doing the many chores daddy use to do for us; trying to make it through till spring. James and I were only eight and ten years old, but we knew mama needed our help just like she needed the older children's help. We grew older and wiser that winter of 1948.

Photo 18. "Dandy Don" and Brother John, 1948.
(Courtesy of Ida Jane Mull Rowland, 2006.)

There was one unique situation in our family for my brother, Donald Roger, which no other child had experienced. He had remained the baby for five years. He had many sisters and brothers surrounding him with love and attention. Daddy often referred to him as "Dandy Don!"

One of Donald's first memories as a child was seeing a man over on the other side of our branch, approaching our farm. Walking across the fields; the stranger wore a black overcoat and a black hat. James ran to tell mama a stranger was coming toward our house. Mama exclaimed, "It is your daddy!" Donald was only three but he remembers mama telling him, "It is your daddy coming home from Canton, Ohio!"

There was no apparent reason for me to do so, but I ran into the house to hide from my daddy. I remember starting to cry and thinking, "Where can I hide?" I quickly opened the door leading upstairs and sat down on the second step.

As I heard daddy greeting every child with a hug and happy comments, I thought, "He will never miss me!" Finally, he asked

"Where is that Eva Nell? Where could she be hiding?" Suddenly, he opened the stairway door and there I sat with my face covered in tears. He reached out his arms and picked me up just like I was a tiny baby. If I live to be a hundred, I will never forget that special hug, the day our daddy came back home. He was smiling and so happy to be back with his family.

Donald recalls, "The happy time at our house was celebrated by hitching up the horses to the wagon and going over to Bob Tiger's Store. There we all got new shoes for winter! We would not have to wear the 'home made' shoes that winter!"

Times were surely going to get better. And they indeed did get better! Daddy bought a 1936 Chevrolet car from Uncle Bryson Mull. Imagine, no more riding in the wagon! We had never, ever had a car before now!

Illustration 9. Daddy's 1936 Chevrolet.

Soon daddy got a job at the Ritter Lumber Company saw mill over in Hayesville. It was a very dangerous job and the pay was low. Daddy sometimes talked about the money he could be making up in Canton, at the steel mills. But mama would not hear to us leaving the Cove and moving to Ohio. She was so happy daddy had a job at home.

Photo 19. *l. to r.* Doc Stanley and Mr. Paul Cunningham
in the Ritter Lumber Yard, circa, 1950.
(Courtesy of Bob Cunningham.)

Everyone was glad to have daddy home with us. I remember waiting every afternoon to see daddy coming home from the saw mill. I loved the way he smelled; all covered in fresh sawdust! He was tired but never as tired as back when he was digging wells for a living.

Daddy worked hard at the mill. His job was what they called 'turning down.' He stood near the carriage which moved the log into the saw. There he would pull the slabs and rough lumber away from the saw onto rollers which moved the lumber products to other parts of the saw mill. It was a very dangerous position! He wore a hard hat and safety glasses but no protection for his hearing.

According to James, "When the log hit that high speed saw the noise was unbelievable! Daddy may not have been aware of the threat to his ability to hear or he may have simply ignored the fact. For seventeen years daddy worked at Ritter Lumber Company. He suffered the rest of his life with a roaring in his ears. His ability to hear was severely damaged."

One summer day in 1948, William brought his girlfriend, Hazel Howell, home for us to meet. She was a very pretty girl! When she asked me to sit beside her on the couch, I was delighted. Later mama said, "William just might marry Miss Hazel!" Well, that is exactly what he did!

They went on a fancy honeymoon and returned in a few weeks for a visit. Hazel said, "Eva Nell, we are going to the Hen Theatre in Murphy. Would you like to go with Bill and me to see a movie?" Well, I just about croaked! First off, the only hen place I knew was the hen house, where I gathered eggs! Secondly, I did not even know what the word movie meant! But straight away, I raced to mama and asked, "Please, please can I go with Hazel and William to Murphy?" Of course she allowed me to go with them. And, of course, I cried through the whole movie. Then I slept all the way home in the back seat of their car.

The next year my sisters, Eddie Lee and Ida Jane got married. Suddenly the house seemed kind of empty without our older sisters. But we still maintained regular visits to our grandparents with the younger children. Now, instead of riding all Sunday afternoon, in the wagon to visit grandma Wimpey and then grandma Mull up on Tusquittee, we could go up in our fancy Chevrolet car.

Things had not changed much up on Tusquittee. Grandpa still sat there after dinner, in a 'straight chair,' on the front porch chewing his tobacco. He had a very precise ritual about cutting off a chew. First he would cut off the store bought tobacco; chew a little bit; then cut himself a plug of his homegrown twist; and put that in his mouth with the store bought chew. Soon he would spit a stream of tobacco juice across the yard! Just like a sharp shooter; he could make a chicken jump real high!

I never did mess around with grandpa's tobacco, which was stored in his log barn behind his house. His Concord grapes were my pick, when it came to passing a wonderful Sunday afternoon at grandpa's house. The same was not true for my brother, James Carl.

It seems that one Sunday afternoon, while I was busy picking grapes, James decided to just explore around the tobacco barn. This led to his thinking it might be good to do a little practice in chewing and spitting like grandpa. James says, "I just knew with some practice I could make those chickens jump - real high! I cut a piece off his home twisted plug and commenced to chew. It didn't take but a few chews until everything begin to turn. My head seemed to be spinning and I had to find a tree to hold. I spit the tobacco out but the sick feeling did not go away very fast. I was able to walk straight by the time we left for home. But I told my dad I just wasn't feeling to well. To this day, for some reason, I have never chewed nor smoked tobacco!"

In early spring, 1950, we all knew that mama was going to have a baby. Sure enough, on April 28, 1950, my mama went to the hospital in Murphy, for her first ever delivery in a hospital. The next day daddy loaded all six of us in his '36 Chevrolet and took us to the hospital to see mama and the new baby boy. She named him David Levoan, in honor of daddy.

Very quietly, we all tiptoed around mama's hospital bed; had a look at our brand new baby brother; and listened to how amazed the nurses were to see all of mama's children! Of course, the older children were not even there! We were enthralled with little David and his blond, cherubic hair. We all got to pat him gently on his head and then daddy took us back home to wait for mama's return.

When mama and the new baby came home, it was Donald who wanted to ask questions. He had been 'our baby' for five years! What was he suppose to do now? Well, of course he wanted to hold the baby, just like everyone else wanted to hold little David. Rather than make Donald wait his turn, Bennie Louise went into the back room and wrapped a doll in a blanket. According to Bennie, Donald did not have just one new baby brother but TWO!

Sitting very carefully in his little rocking chair, Donald was handed the 'baby/doll.' Bennie told him to be very careful with the baby. Watching Donald gently rocking the baby; Bennie finally suggested that Donald remove the blanket and look at the second 'new baby.' Well, to recall the look of disappointment and shock written on Donald's face, to this day, still brings peels of laughter to my sister, Bennie. There is no telling what Donald Roger thinks of her trickery!

Lest the memories of our childhood experiences of going to church by horse-drawn wagon slip away; we can always refer to the words written by a dear friend, Mrs. Mabel Kitchens, in February, 1977; as published in the "Clay County Progress News."

"Sunday afternoon was a happy occasion at Hinton Center. Mr. and Mrs. Joe Mull celebrated their 50th wedding anniversary. I want to say' Congratulations' to one of the finest couples I know. Mr. and Mrs. Mull are special in my book. They have raised eleven fine children and both enjoy good health. I always look forward to seeing them when I go to the Hayesville Church of God. I know right where they sit and I know they will be there to fill their place.

I was talking with Mrs. Grace Mease, Sunday afternoon, as she said, 'When I was just a little girl the thing that impressed me about Uncle Joe and Aunt Martha most was the fact the weather never got too bad for him to hook his team to the wagon and take their family to church. They set a fine example before their children.'"

Chapter 7

Spreading Our Wings

By the time I had entered eighth grade, in the Clay County, NC Schools, it was evident that I should be learning from my older siblings. The greatest lesson for me came from observing my sister, Bennie Louise. She was fortunate to be invited to play basketball by the coach, Mrs. Laura McGlamery.

One day Mrs. Mac gave Bennie a basketball uniform and asked her to play on the team. She very proudly took the uniform home and asked her father's permission to play on the team. The next day Bennie took the uniform back and tried to give it to Mrs. Mac. With a very heavy heart, she explained that her father would not allow her to wear the uniform due to our religious beliefs.

Mrs. Mac knew very well that our sister Eddie Lee had not been permitted to play basketball. Being a diplomatic and determined coach, Mrs. Mac told Bennie, "Keep the uniform and I will go talk to your father!" She did so and Bennie was allowed to join the basketball team.

As the season passed Bennie's basketball skills were honed to a high level. It was evident to Mrs. Mac that Bennie was a very talented and enthusiastic player. However, Bennie secretly dreaded the 'road trips' for the away games. It seemed to Bennie that the other girls always had money to buy food and drinks on the road trips. Of course there was no money for Bennie to buy food! Yet, somewhere along the way Mrs. Mac would very discreetly place a couple of dollar bills in Bennie's hand. This kindness was not lost on our family. I knew that basketball would be my passion in high school!

Mrs. Mac soon recruited my sister, Mary Jo, for her team. Then through a most incredible stroke of luck, Mrs. Mac decided to invite me to come up from the eighth grade to play on her team. Today I can still remember how my heart was pounding when she called to me; "Mull, go to the free throw line and shoot a couple." At home I had been hitting foul shots easily at our goal in the back yard. But this was different. This was for Mrs. Mac!

I managed to hit a couple of shots and she just nodded her head. I knew I had made it! The dedication with which I played basketball for Mrs. Mac resulted in my teammates voting me Captain of our team in my senior year. I felt so fortunate and honored to have been selected for such a distinction.

My mother and father never came to a single one of our basketball games. Yet, we knew in the long run they were proud of our effort. Daddy would often come home with news from the 'Square' about how great his daughters played basketball. We loved our 'fans' and their kind words about our performance. This was just one of many times in my life that I felt lucky to be number seven in a long line of children.

As Bennie approached her senior year at Hayesville High School, she and her friend, Pee Wee Brooks, decided they would join the United States Air Force. When she announced this plan to my parents, it did not fly! My mother, in her firm and emphatic style, said "I would rather see you in your grave than to see you make that choice!" That was the end of the discussion. Bennie changed her plans.

Attending college was certainly not on the table for discussion. As Bennie Louise heard her name called on graduation night; to come forth and receive her high school diploma from Hayesville High School; she knew very well what was coming up next. She was going to leave all her friends and her dear teachers, whom she had grown to love over the past twelve years.

But the hardest part was yet to come! She was going to leave her mother and father and all her brothers and sisters. According to Bennie, "In some ways, it was terrifying! Then I looked upon it as another milestone I had reached in my life. I had received $50.00 for graduation. I thought I had plenty of money!"

During those closing months of the school year, I had watched closely how Bennie approached her final days with us. I could not believe she would leave us! On graduation night her suitcase was packed and so carefully placed on the front porch.

As she made her way across the small porch and told us all "Goodbye" I tried very hard to not let the tears flow. Then in a minute she was gone! The night was long. For days I was very heavy hearted. I knew, someday, I also would have to make such an exodus. I did not know how, but I knew the day would come when I would leave the Cove.

For Bennie, spreading her wings and leaving the Cove, with $50.00 in her pocket, turned into an eighteen hour trip; by car through the mountains with many a curve; on her way to Canton, Ohio. Today she recalls, "I had always heard daddy talk about going to Canton, when times were so tough and being able to find a good job. Now I was on my way! I was on my way to a new place, a good job and new friends."

Through her weekly letters home, we learned Bennie indeed had gotten a good job in Canton. We were so proud of her! Every month she would send $4.00 home to pay for piano lessons for her sister, Nancy Sue. Bennie never mentioned being home sick.

The months passed and things did not seem to change much in my tenth year of school. I still missed not having Bennie Louise in the house. Times were still hard and winter weather seemed to rush upon us; even before my daddy had been able to finish repairing our cold weather shoes. Summer shoes seemed to be imaginary. Although every once in a while one of the daughters got a pretty pair of sandals. If the sandals did not wear out too quickly, I just might get to wear them.

My mama was writing to Bennie quiet regularly. In early 1954, my grandmother Wimpey passed away and my mama was so sad. I thought her sorrow would kill her. After grandmother Wimpey's funeral, my mama wrote a letter to Bennie, saying, "Dear Bennie Louise, today we buried my mother." That was about the saddest letter Bennie ever received. She loved her grandmother Wimpey very much! We all did! We had all stayed, at one time or another, with grandma and helped take care of her when she was low sick.

I remember thinking, "How sad Bennie must be way up north and unable to come back for the funeral." A lot of good things could be written about my grandmother. But I guess it would be fair to say grandma returned our love a thousand fold.

In the spring things kind of lightened up for our sister, Bennie. She wrote home that she had a new boyfriend who was nice. His name was Bill Yaus and we could tell she liked him very much! She said, "I love spending time with Bill and we have even talked about coming to North Carolina, for a vacation."

Whoa! This could be the start of something really big for us. Not a big bang, but in the back of my mind I was just doing a little thinking. If 'getting a job' in Canton, Ohio, was so easy for Bennie, then maybe, just maybe somebody else could 'get a job' in Canton! I never mentioned a word about my future plans to anyone. I just laid low and prepared for the big celebration, when Bennie would come home with her new beau! I simply could not wait!

Up to this point in our childhood the only games we had ever played was Knocking the Tin Can, Tap Hand, Pitching Horse Shoe,

Basketball, or There Ain't No Bugger Bears Out to Night. Now it seemed this new boyfriend had other plans for us. He agreed to come down and visit in the Cove, if he could stop in Tennessee, and get some firecrackers.

Bennie thought, "Well, why not just have a little fun with my brothers?" She knew very well daddy did not put up with 'foolishness' like shooting firecrackers. Yet she really did want to come for a visit!

Upon the arrival of Bennie and her boyfriend, Bill, we were so happy to see them. However it was Sunday morning and time to go to church. Mama decided maybe the boys could stay home and enjoy getting to know the 'nice' young man, whom Bennie had brought down from Ohio.

Well, there was exactly where the real trouble started! Mama and daddy disappeared from view, with me and the little ones, on our way to church. Heaven help Donald and James! They had been left behind with this 'stranger' in their midst!

Bill decided that they ought to get busy shooting the firecrackers he had purchased in Tennessee. He did not know daddy's rule, that one does not shoot firecrackers ANY day in the week, let alone on Sunday! Yet knowing this fact, James and Donald pushed the rule right out of their minds. They were just jumping with glee as Bill shot the first few firecrackers.

As he kept shooting the firecrackers, he decided to ask the boys to find a can to put over the firecrackers. That way they could get a bigger bang. Well, James promptly ran and got one of our tin cans. That worked for a couple of explosions. Then a request was made for a big bucket to get a bigger bang!

It has never been determined which son, James or Donald, actually went to the hog lot and got daddy's big feed bucket. But that was their downfall! That bucket would later provide real 'evidence' looming over their heads. It happened in a split second; the really BIG BANG; which Bill had promised them! The big bucket, which was daddy's favorite bucket, went up in the air with a mighty explosion and down it fell to the ground. Bill thought it was a really good show for the boys.

Sadly, James and Donald viewed the condition of the feed bucket. The bottom was rounded and ruined. Then they thought of their own bottoms. What were they going to do? When was church going to be over? Was it too late to pray? Was the blast which took the bucket twenty feet into the air really worth it? Suddenly, this new Yankee fellow, who talked so fast, just seemed to have ruined the bucket and their peaceful Sunday morning.

Well, finally the worried boys saw the car coming around the Cove, and Daddy was in the driver's seat! They knew their time had come. The round bottom bucket was all they had to show for their morning of 'disobeying' their father. James whispered to his younger brother, "This is not going to set well with daddy!" Donald ask, "What do you mean, not set well with daddy? We can hammer it out real quick!" James responded in a sad tone, "Nope, it's too late now!"

Arriving home with mama and daddy, I quickly went inside the house. One glance at Donald and James made me realize my place was in the house helping mama. I did not want to see the fur fly! Plus, I wanted to get on with my business of figuring out how to ask mama if I could go to Ohio, with Bennie Louise.

Pretty soon daddy came in the house looking mighty grim and unhappy about something. I was kind of worried. But when we sat down to a fine dinner of chicken and dumplings, I knew everything was going to be fine. I knew Bill Yaus had met with mama's approval. She had prepared a dinner fit for a preacher man! Shore 'nuff, everything was going to be alright!

After Sunday dinner, I went to washing dishes like 'nobody's business' and hoping Bennie would help me. She always helped me with the dishes back when she was still at home. Surely, surely she would help me on this special Sunday.

Shore 'nuff, she came right into the kitchen and starting drying the dishes for me. That was when I ask her the question; "Can I please go to Ohio, with you and get a job? I have got to buy my class ring, pay for my typing, and lots of other things! Please say yes and ask mama for me, please?" No time passed till Bennie said, "You can go back with us if mama says so."

Whoa! This Yankee boyfriend was not so bad! Mama gave her permission with much reluctance. The only hitch, which slowed my departure, was a broken axle on that fancy 1951, two-toned, vinyl top Ford they were driving.

That Bill got busy! He pulled that bad axle out that car; took it to the junk yard; and got a replacement for almost nothing. Finally, daddy was impressed with Bennie's new boyfriend! All of a sudden that feed bucket seemed like a small matter. The firecrackers were gone with the wind!

I packed my little suitcase and was out of the Cove with my sister, Bennie, even before I had time to get sad! I was bound for Ohio, with a birth certificate indicating I was eighteen years old. The long, curvy trip just flew by and we were way up into flatland by sunrise. I never slept a wink the whole way.

Returning to the Cove on a Greyhound bus bound for Murphy, was one happy day in my life! I will never forget that trip! Thanks to Bennie, I had $600.00 in my pocket. She had not allowed me to pay one red cent for rent, buy food or anything else while I was working in Canton. She made me save every penny. Now, I could pay all my school expenses for my junior year of high school. Plus, I would have spending money for away basketball games.

The first thing I did after getting back to the Cove was place an order to Sears Roebuck for a 'new' winter coat. I can still remember opening the package. Finally, I had received my very own, first ever, new coat by mail! It fit perfectly!

I will never forget that beautiful blue wool overcoat. The only other new item I could ever remember getting before in my whole life was a new dress my mama sewed on her Singer, for my tenth birthday. It was made from flour sacks but it was fine and dandy! It was mine; hand made by my mama!

My junior year of school passed by and soon the summer was approaching. I began to make my plans to go to Atlanta, Georgia. Many girls had gone down to Atlanta, and gotten good jobs. I knew I could make it. I headed to Sears Roebuck & Company, on Ponce de Leon Avenue. I had my birth certificate showing me to be nineteen years old. On the job application I indicated I had graduated from high school. My typing skills were good and the job was mine!

I worked very hard at Sears. In the autumn, I told my boss I had to go home and help mama with the younger children. That was the *truth*! The senior year was upon me and I was not ready to make the break. I was not ready to leave my family and the Cove for good!

Many of the 'town girls' were getting ready to go away to college. Like all my sisters, I knew college was not an option. During my four years in high school I had focused on basketball instead of academics. Even though my daddy had told us so many times how important it was to 'get a good education,' I had no hope of continuing my education. So I departed the Cove for the last time! I was off to Atlanta! This time I was going to find a permanent job.

I found work at Southern Bell Telephone Company, on Ivy Street. Like many girls from Hayesville, my world began to expand beyond my family and the Cove. But I did not forget how Benny had sent money home to pay for Nancy Sue's piano lessons. I vowed, "That is exactly what I will do for my brother, Donald Roger!" Today when he tells me how delighted he was back then, that I 'remembered him,' it brings me much happiness.

Chapter 8

Long Journey Home

How to deal with death and dying was one lesson I did not learn very well, growing up in the Matheson Cove. The care and guidance provided by our parents kept us safe. They kept close watch over us. Their sad stories were shared so many times as we sat around the fireplace in the front room. 'Little Jessie' and 'Little Onas' were names of our uncles who had passed away as teenagers. Of course, loosing our grandparents was a lesson in living and dying. Somehow that seemed a perfectly natural thing. As I had learned through the teachings of my mother; "It is appointed unto man, once to die."

As children, whispering upstairs when we were suppose to be sleeping; I remember our hushed conversations about death. My main fear was of our house burning down. Every night daddy would cover the burning embers in our fireplace with ashes. If I were awake and downstairs still talking with daddy, he would explain how one must be very careful with the fireplace. In his words, "I have known about many a family perishing because their house burned down!"

Many years later, living over in Tennessee, we had no open fireplace in our house. We had gas logs! We were safe and we had a perfectly happy life with our sons, Jimmy and Joey. {James Seymour Wike, Jr. (b. 07-09-61), Joseph Howard Wike (b. 06-03-65; d. 06-06-82)} Of course I was following the lessons I had learned from my parents. We thought our sons would grow up to be fine, up-standing good men. But that was not to be for our Joey.

On a beautiful Sunday afternoon, three days after Joey had turned seventeen years old; he was killed in a car accident. As we learned of his death, my dear husband accepted the earth shaking news with incredible calmness.

My world was shattered and still is today. However, as we have somehow moved through these many years of learning and living without Joey, I feel a keen sense of maturity. And even a tiny bit of understanding about how to deal with a child's death.

After Joey's death I tried to go back to the classroom to teach the mathematics. I had been tutoring him in the same level of Algebra. The first few weeks of being back in the classroom seemed to be pure agony. It was impossible for me to be among those wonderful teenage students who reminded me so much of Joey.

One day while doing my 'hall duty,' I overheard two students talking. One said, "She just stands there and stares into space. Do you think she is crazy?" I did not look at the young girl who had asked the question. I just knew it was time for me to leave the school. I loved teaching. I could not fail! Failure was NOT going to be the way a Mull girl from the Matheson Cove was going to be remembered.

On the Sunday evening Joey died, I did not telephone anyone. No one in my family knew of the accident. The long night passed into dawn. At daybreak, I folded his robe and put it away. Then I phoned my sister, Mary Jo. Her daughter, Angela, answered. The news went out to all members of my family.

They all made that long journey to Tennessee. I said to my mother, "You came for his birth and now you come for his death!" Standing in front of the casket with my mother and father, I recalled their stories around the fireplace about little Onus and little Jessie. Surely, I could get past Joey's death.

My youngest brother, David, was serving in the U. S. Army and could not be in Tennessee. At the funeral, my family and Jim's family walked slowly into the Sanctuary of the First United Methodist Church and sat down. They filled almost half the pews on one side of the Sanctuary. Later a friend said to me, "Eva, it was like an army coming into the Church. Your family just kept on coming down the aisle. How many brothers and sisters do you have, anyway?"

The next week David called me. He said, "Now, Eva we want you to get well!" I told him the story of our family entering the church 'like an army' and filling many church pews. I said, "Maybe I can get well for my family." He quickly replied, "Not for our family! For you! Eva, you must get well for yourself!"

I sought refuge in Charlotte, teaching in a big high school; living for three months with Mary Jo's family; then three months with Bennie Louise's family. At the end of the school term, I knew I was not 'out of the woods' yet.

That summer an AFS student from Australia came to visit us in Oak Ridge. She asked, "When are you coming to Australia, Eva?" It suddenly hit me! That would be a solution! I just knew Australia would be a good place to sit in the burning sun and let my heart heal.

My husband, in his most understanding manner, asked, "Do I have to go?" I replied, "Of coursc, you do!" Then he inquired, "Well, what about work? Do you want me to quit my job, too?"

After sitting on a sugar cane farm in Australia, for two months, I returned to Oak Ridge. I knew I had to finish my doctorate degree from the University of Tennessee, and get a job. Life had to go on! How do you do these things with a broken heart and a broken mind?

At home as a child, I was famous for having my very own 'crying post' out on the back porch. But those days were gone. I could not be sad the rest of my life! Well, where do you go when you can not think but in sad, sad terms?

You go where they sing sad songs! You go to Nashville! That is exactly where I went to teach in a fantastic high school, for fifteen years. So many times I made that long journey home to Oak Ridge. I really do not know how I got up the courage and energy to become a good teacher and make a contribution to the lives of so many young students.

Finally, I felt a sense of happiness and strength like I had never felt in my life. When I retired from teaching in the year 2000, I had three wonderful grandsons who were going to occupy my world. My mission would be to make it beautiful for them.

Now, I really know about 'rough' times! I am a long way from being an expert, but my stories are honest and heartfelt. You have my blessings and permission to cry in the stories that follow - on our long journey home.

From Past to Present

Life is so sublime at times. Recently, I was sitting at the old home place, over in the Cove. Sitting around our campfire with my brothers and sister; just singing and listening to Jim play his harmonica; it seemed the old place had never been more peaceful.

My dear sister-in-law, Brenda Mull, commented, "You know this is so perfect! Here we are singing in grandma's garden, just like she was still with us." The thought went through my mind, "Nope, if mama was still here we would be working in this garden, not singing in it!" But I pushed the thought away and quickly agreed this was going to be our perfect October weekend.

Our singing, cooking on the burning embers and recalling 'the good old days' went on as the full moon rose over the garden. We all felt the chill of autumn in the air but we did not want to say "Good Night!"

The next day the call came from Brenda's son, Ronnie. My brother, James, answered the phone and moved too quickly outside on the front porch. In a moment he stepped to the door and called "Brenda" in a voice which seemed too loud. Brenda quickly moved to the porch to take the phone.

After too many minutes, James came to the door. He really did not have to say a word. I had picked up all 'the signs' before he ever announced that Brenda's nephew, at age 48, had just died suddenly of a heart attack. Hastily Brenda and James moved through the house with their luggage. They could not hide their tears. Then they were gone!

We all sat around kind of stunned. Jim made the comment, "Isn't it strange how we can't feel other people's pain?" Our response was just silence. In the early evening we went back to the garden. Donald built a fire. He insisted we roast the hotdogs and maybe sing a little bit. We may not have felt Brenda's pain when she received the telephone call, but we sure were not doing much singing that evening.

The full moon rose high once again over the garden, just like it had the previous night. My unspoken thoughts were on sadder times. We sat in silence and looked at the full moon. I was lost in my own recollections. Joey had been born on a full, June moon. He had died on that same full moon, seventeen years later. Then, I remembered a call I had received from Bennie on January 29, 1989, in Nashville.

So quickly, I felt the earthshaking sadness envelope me that cold January evening; even before Bennie finished saying "Eva?" Feeling my body start to shake, I knew someone had died! She continued, "Jason went diving and didn't make it." My next response was not logical. "Not my brother!" I said. She hesitated, and then softly she replied, "Yes, Don and Darlene have lost their son, Jason!"

I had spent lots of sad nights in Nashville. But that night I felt so down and alone. The next morning I was shaking so I could not talk. I had to write a note to my Principal, explaining why I needed to leave school for two days. She responded, "Go, Dr. Wike. Stay as long as you like!" I managed to say, "No, I will be back tomorrow." With a look of surprise on her face, she said, "You mean you are not going to stay for the services?" I replied, "If I stay for the services I will not be able to drive back." She seemed to understand.

Quickly I entered the ramp on the Interstate and was able to start my long journey to Lawrenceville, Ga. Somehow I was able to get to Chattanooga, and meet Jim. He drove on to Donald and Darlene's house. When we knocked, Darlene met us at the door with a tearful smile on her face. The thought went through my mind, "You are doing good, girl!" I ask, "Where is Don?" She whispered softly, "He is upstairs."

I knew he was not sleeping. I knew he was aching with pain like he had never known. Slowly I went upstairs to Don. We just sat there on his big king-size bed and cried like babies. We did not have to say a word. I knew the hard road he had ahead of him. I knew he would make it! He had faced harsh times with two tours of military duty in Vietnam, which he had survived. I knew he was too strong to stay down forever!

Coming back to the full moon rising over mama's garden; I tried to focus on the 'garden talk' and enjoy the beautiful moment. But my thoughts went back to Brenda and James. It was so true that with the death of our handsome teenage sons, Donald and I had somehow shared our sorrow. But what about James and Brenda's infant son, Roger Carl Mull (b.; d. 8-4-71) who never lived one day? Do we have a place in our hearts for their sorrowful times so long ago? Indeed, we must!

Whether we have lost a teenage son, an infant son or a grown up brother, we must keep a place in our heart for them. As I recall my older brother, John (b. 07-03-1931; d. 10-30-1991), I remember him as a kind hearted boy who had difficulty in school. Book learning may not have interested him. After twenty-five years of classroom experiences, I have a much deeper appreciation for John's hard times in school.

My sister, Bennie Louise, often shared precious memories about John. He loved his brothers and sisters! Bennie told how John once brought money to her house. He asked her to please buy flowers and send them to the funeral of our sister-in-law, Hazel Howell Mull. At John's death, Bennie sure stood strong for our family.

That October day, as Bennie was preparing for John's funeral, I had rented a fancy car and driven to the Cove. My mission was to make sure my mother and father would travel in comfort to their son's funeral. As I gently helped daddy pull his soft blue sweater over his shoulders, the phone rang. The call was from my brother, David, who was preparing to board a plane in Texas, to come to John's funeral in Gaston County, NC.

Mama answered the phone and I watched as her face grew even sadder and her eyes filled with tears. Not saying a word, she handed me the phone and David said, "Eva, I told mama if she brings daddy down to John's funeral, we'll have two funerals to attend. Daddy can't make it!

We would not be down in Gaston County for John's funeral. We would sit silently in the front room, watching the hands of the clock move slowly toward the hour for John's service. Bennie had done her best. I could surely sit there with my parents and just listen to the clock tick away the hour.

The Clock of Life

The clock of life is wound but once
And no man has the power
To tell just when the hands will stop
At late or early hour.

So, now is the time to live and to
Love with a will!
Place no faith in tomorrow
For the hands may then be still.

Dixie Wiggins Farley, 1931

Following John's death, my father was with us only a few short months. Daddy had been a strong man and enjoyed all aspects of life. But one thing about it, he did not like being down. At the Hiawassee Hospital, where he was a patient, I listened as daddy questioned his physician about his recovery. I saw the look on the doctor's face and I knew daddy had 'read' the doctor's face just like I had read it. I observed the look on my father's face. I had never ever, in my whole life, seen my father 'give up!' But I think that day daddy gave up.

Daddy lived on about twenty more days in his hospital room. I had the great fortune to spend his last weekend on earth with him. The weather was perfect and without anyone's permission I asked my father if he wanted to take a stroll outside. He gave me the sweetest smile, like he always did when I came over from Tennessee. I expected him to say, "No, honey!" But he did not. He just said, "Sure, honey! If you think that it is all right!" I assured him it would be fine.

As we 'strolled' outside with daddy sitting secured in a wheel chair, he looked about the sunny setting. Then he gave me that mischievous grin and said, "This would be a nice place to get married!" I giggled and said, "But daddy, you are already married to mama!" We talked about the locust tree growing below the plaza. I recalled how he and I use to walk in the woods. Back then he had taught me the names and uses of all the trees. My time with him was over! We went back inside and called a nurse to help us. Leaving him that weekend, I knew I would never talk to my daddy again.

As we buried my father, on a beautiful Father's Day, June 18, 1992, his funeral services lasted all day. So many people wanted to express their most endearing thoughts about our father. Wonderful folks sang his favorite songs. I felt it was a funeral like some 'royal' person would have received at their burial. During our 6:00 p.m. evening meal daddy's dear sister, Aunt Lillie, entered the fellowship hall of Shady Grove Baptist Church. It was a peaceful ending!

Peace In The Valley
(Thomas A. Dorsey, 1939)

Well, I'm tired and so weary but I must go along
Till the Lord comes and calls me away, oh yes
Where the morning's so bright and the Lamb is the light
And the night is as bright as the day, oh yes!

There will be peace in the valley for me some day
There will be peace in the valley for me, oh Lord I pray
There'll be no sadness, no sorrow, and no trouble I see
There will be peace in the valley for me!

There the flowers will be blooming and the grass will be green
And the skies will be clear and serene, oh yes
The sun ever beams in this valley of dreams
And no cloud will ever be seen, oh yes!

Later that day, as we were saying goodbye to everyone standing on the front porch at home, I saw my mother surrounded by her children. They would all soon depart and I imagined her standing alone on the porch. How could she bare the stark lonely times ahead?

Suddenly, my brother David said, "Now, mama, this would be a good time for you to come to Oklahoma for a visit. Don't you think so, Eva?" Quickly I responded, "Why it sure would, but that is a long way for mama to ride!" He replied, "But there are airplanes, you know. You have flown all over the world! You could fly with mama, couldn't you? "Yes, of course," I replied, "If mama will fly, I will take her to Oklahoma, sure as I'm standing here!" In my heart I knew my mama would just say "No!" Suddenly, the brightest smile moved across her face as she nodded her hcad yes. Then I knew she and I were bound for Oklahoma!

The airport in Atlanta may not be the biggest airport in the world. But that day of departure, I was sure it was the biggest and the only airport my mother had ever visited. My brothers and sisters had kindly brought mama down from the Cove, and we were ready to make her 'maiden voyage' to Oklahoma. Mama was cooler than a cucumber! The same could not be said for me or my siblings. But we managed to get through the process of departure, saying our farewells a dozen times.

The sights and sounds we experienced on the plains of Oklahoma, surely impressed my mama. Mama loved seeing all the prairie dogs and buffalo. She laughed and joked about her Buffalo nickel she had kept since she was a little girl. We enjoyed visiting museums, driving through the Fort Sill Army Base, seeing the countryside and touring the Capitol building in Oklahoma City. The Native American exhibits we saw in the museums reminded me of that terrible exodus for the Cherokee Nation. I did not have the heart to discuss it with mama.

While in the airport getting ready to depart, mama suddenly stopped and looked at something nearby. I ask, "What is it mama?" She said, "Look over there! Honey, I do believe those steps are moving!" I patted her hand and said, "Indeed they are, mama! You really have good eyes. But we are going to use the elevator, because I am afraid of those moving steps."

Later that evening, making our approach to the Atlanta airport, I felt a keen sense of having accomplished the impossible. Then suddenly a thunder storm struck like no other thunder storm! Lightening flashed; the plane went into turbulence; and l started thinking about 'the bag.'

After just a few minutes of the turbulence, the pilot came on and announced we would be climbing to a higher altitude; getting out of the turbulence and waiting for the storm to pass. I thought about my brothers and sisters down there on the ground waiting for mama to get down. On and on we circled that dang airport!

Just when I was about to start wringing my hands, I turned to mama and said, "Hang on mama, maybe, maybe the pilot will get us down soon." She smiled her 'well traveled' smile and said, "Honey, don't worry! The Good Lord will help him land it!" And, He did! Neither one of us got motion sickness, but I was still shaking long after my feet touched the ground.

Today I am still amazed at how calmly my mother faced my father's passing. I have often recalled her sorrow at the time of granny Wimpey's death. Maybe she had grown stronger in her aging years because of the losses she had experienced. I never talked about such a notion with my mother.

It had been one decade between Joey's death and my father's death. It was at this juncture in my life that I decided it was time for me to face the world. I had hidden my sorrow and loss long enough. By talking with friends in Nashville; who had suffered great emotional pain I found solace. Somehow, I would find a place to lay my burden down. After much time and meditation, I knew my peace would be found in my gardens, alone!

Ode to Winter Gardens

As these falling needles and leaves speak of Return
Their long labor of green turned finally into Gold,
The desire that remembered him in this Place
Is now prepared to let him go.

Though not for want of faithfulness! All that once
Followed the full moon, still follows it now,
As it slips away, she folds his robe by daybreak
And enters the soundless gardens hidden under
The snow.

Eva M. Wike, Ph.D.
Winter, 1992

For almost another decade, my mother was at peace at the old home place. We visited her often in the Cove and came over any time we were needed for a weekend. It was tough coming up from Nashville, to Oak Ridge, and then on over to Hayesville. But all her children provided support and my mother did well for awhile.

As she grew weaker and things got more complicated in providing her with the support she needed, we made the very tough decision for her to go to a care center. She finally adjusted and seemed at peace with the care and our frequent visits.

In June, 2002, Jim and I visited her. He played the piano and we tried to sing. It was pretty awful but we laughed a lot and had fun. When I got ready to leave, I said, "Mama, I am going on a walking tour of Normandy, way over in France. I will be gone a few weeks." She seemed to follow my conversation. Smiling, she replied, "Well, Honey, I hope you have a good trip." Departing, I whispered to my mother, "I'll be back in July!"

As Jim and I walked out, me in tears of course, I said, "That's my last meaningful conversation with my mother!" At the end of July, sorrow hit us again. On a Thursday, I got the call from Jane, "Mother fell this morning and she is in the hospital!" I responded, "I will be over in the morning and stay all weekend. Maybe you and Eddie Lee can have a good weekend."

By Sunday, my mother had faded like a flower; going from a weak smile on Friday to almost no response on Sunday morning. While I waited for James and Brenda to come, my brother, William, came to visit mama. We stood there and looked at our mother, so still and pale. He whispered, "Death would be a blessing!" I shivered and turned away. Soon William departed and I starting 'walking the floors.'

First I would go to my mother's bed and put ice on her lips. Then I would walk to the door and cry. I did not want to cry in front of her.

But she would have never known! After several back and forth trips from her bed to the doorway, a nurse came to me and asked, "Can I do something for you, honey?" Sobbing, I responded, "No! I am telling my mother goodbye." The nurse said, "Oh, don't say that! She might do all right."

Soon Brenda and James came and I started my long journey back to Tennessee. By the time I reached Sweetwater, my tears had dried. I was so glad mama had not died while I was with her. Bennie Louise and Bill came the next day and stayed three nights with my mother. They celebrated their wedding anniversary as they sat by her bedside.

Early in the morning of their last day, they heard my mother make a gasping sound and they called the nurse. Quietly the nurse checked and then whispered to my sister, Bennie, "Your mother is gone, Honey."

A Private Moment

As we entered Ivey's Funeral Home on a warm August afternoon, my husband kindly stayed behind as I walked alone into the receiving room. It was still and quiet. My mother looked so beautiful. I recalled a memory from my childhood, when a little friend in church service had whispered to me, "Your mother is so pretty!" Indeed she was, in life and in death! I gently placed the huge basket arrangement of flowers, which Jimmy and Catherine had sent. I thought of one of mama's favorite songs:

> "Give me the roses while I live
> Trying to cheer me on
> Useless the flowers that you give
> After the soul is gone."

Finally, Jim came in and we just stood there for a long time in silence. It had been so meaningful to have just a few last moments alone with my mama.

The funeral service for my mother was just as moving as that which we had experienced for my father. As I left the funeral home, I turned to hug my Aunt Mary Mease. Aunt Mary is my mother's last sibling. She was born in 1904, and at age 101, she is very bright and cheerful.

When I want to be reminded of my mother's smile and funny stories, I go visit Aunt Mary and her daughter, Sarah. Sometimes I take a whole bunch of my brothers and sisters to visit with Aunt Mary. We fill up her whole living room but she does not mind. Sharing family photos and wonderful stories about "Mary and Martha" makes my heart light.

Chapter 9

Return to the Matheson Cove

In early November, I do not have to be in the Matheson Cove to imagine the Sun easing up from behind Standing Indian Mountain. So many times I have stood at my mother's kitchen window and watched this 'moving' solar art exhibit. The changing colors flowing across at sunrise would drive any artist crazy, trying to capture the tapestry of views on canvas.

Yesterday was my sister, Eddie Lee's birthday. James Carl will soon be celebrating his birthday. Mama always loved this time of year when the ridges would take on their autumn brilliance. I can almost see her now, standing out on the front porch and saying, "Look at those ridges! They're so pretty!"

It is good to recall a hot August day when we were sitting on the porch visiting with mama and daddy. I was telling daddy of our plans to do some hiking on the Trail and camping upon Standing Indian. Shaking his head, daddy asked, "Why are you going to do that, Honey?" I responded, "Because, you never would take us girls hiking up there like you did the boys! And besides, next month I will be 50 years old. I just want to see if I can do it." I will never forget his slow, encouraging nod and reply, "You can do it!"

That was a long time ago, before our beautiful Clay County had been advertised all over creation by the use of 'cyberspace.' I rue the day that strangers discovered the least populated and most picturesque county in our great state of North Carolina. When will this 'overrun' stop?

Now, why am I concerned about our changing ridges in the Matheson Cove? Why do I feel so strongly about preserving those ridges? Well, frankly, I do not want to see them change! The tops of those ridges have remained unchanged for ages! It remained unchanged long after the Cherokee Indians were driven from their campsites along the branch that flows out of the Cross-Tie Holler.

In the summertime, as children, we use to explore those campsites. We found many treasures, such as pottery and arrowheads, near the branch. Daddy assured us, "It was once the place where Indians children played, but they had long since departed!" To us it was indeed a special place!

Along the banks of the stream my sisters and I would build our imaginary big houses on the very *soft-carpeted* floor of the forest. We outlined our big rooms with special stones we carefully selected from the branch. Of course, sometimes the 'wild Indians' came and tore up our playhouse. But the next day we would be right back in the forest again building our big playhouse.

In our wildest imagination, we would never have thought that someday real big houses would be built on the tops of those ridges. Why would anyone seek to build on the highest points? Destroying the most trees; putting in the steepest roads; creating erosion and contaminating our ground water; and simply spoiling our environment in the Cove? It is stupefying to me! Perhaps I am simple minded and ill informed. Maybe I do not exactly understand what progress means to the good folks in the Cove.

A September to Remember!

In my back yard, here in Oak Ridge, the witch hazel is in full bloom. It reminds me of my last trip up into the Cove with my parents in the autumn of 1991.

Photo 20. Hamamelis x Witch Hazel, 'Diana.'
(Courtesy of Eva Nell Mull Wike, 2006.)

That special weekend I had driven up from Nashville, to Oak Ridge, and on over to Hayesville, for a September visit. While talking to daddy about this beautiful witch hazel shrub; which I had seen blooming in Nashville; he told me that witch hazel grew wild along the branch up in the Cove. He reckoned if we went up to Mr. Garcia's house we might be able to find it.

Daddy was very weak but we gently helped him into the car and drove up in the Cove. After Mr. Garcia got over his shock of seeing me standing there on his driveway, 'looking for witch hazel,' he agreed to hike down to the branch with me and look for the shrub. Daddy and mama sat in the car enjoying the unexpected excursion to the Cove. Mr. Garcia and I traipsed back and forth, carrying twigs for daddy to look at and hopefully declare that we indeed had found a witch hazel shrub.

Daddy and mama laughed and joked about 'revenuers' being in the woods. But soon we had to thank Mr. Garcia and go back home with empty hands; just like the revenuers! Helping daddy back into his chair in the front room, I had the greatest desire to simply hold on to this memory forever!

Now, fifteen years later, as I view my witch hazel, looking so special in my back yard, my mind is drawn back to the Cove. Those new homes popping up along the ridges just seem out of place up there. Shaving off the tops of those beautiful mountains and paving over those old home sites is just a shame in my book! It seems like an insult to both the memory of the old folks and the environment.

Surely, we must provide our descendents with some kind of appreciation and understanding of this beloved Cove. It is only through our stories, our music and preservation of our way of life, that our grandchildren will know their heritage. I will declare the destruction of our ridges is not the way to preserve the things we cherish!

A Memorial to a Grand Old Mountain

To the death of what has always been,
A favorite place of mine.
The proud old Shewbird Mountain,
Above my home in Caroline.
I'll not forget those cold clear springs,
Flowing from the rocks above.
They run down into the valley,
Of a land I'll always love.
Those cold dark caves and the old slick rock,
I played on as a lad,
Remind me of my childhood days,
And all the fun I had.
There's so much in that mountain's heart,
Besides grey granite stone.
For this is where I found my peace,
With nature all along.
I've felt a lot of memories
In that old mountain's face.
It breaks my heart to see it go,
And lose all its grace.
I've loved that mountain all my life,
And will until I die.
And as I watch my memories crushed,
I try hard not to cry.
I'll not forget this grand old place,
Throughout the coming years.
And before I'm dead I know I'll shed
At least a million tears.
Good-bye old friend!

Poet: Jack Douglas Matheson
Matheson Cove, Hayesville, NC
Previously published in the
"Clay County Progress News."

Photo 21. The Shewbird Mountain dying a 'man-made' death!
(Courtesy of Donna Moncrief Mull, 2006.)

Photo 22. 'Sight' on the other side of the Shewbird Mountain!
(Courtesy of Eva Nell Mull Wike, 2006.)

Photo 23. Burying the 'REMAINS' of the Shewbird!
(Courtesy of Eva Nell Mull Wike, 2006.)

Photo 24. Washing away the good Red Earth!
(Courtesy of Eva Nell Mull Wike, 2006.)

Photo 25. Do we need this 'Cat' crawling along our ridges?
(Courtesy of Eva Nell Mull Wike, 2006.)

Bibliography

1. Wimpey, George A. *The History of the Wimpey Family of Hayesville, North Carolina*, (Unpublished document, 1993).
2. Jensen, Jane *CHOESTOE "Where the Rabbits Play,"* (Unpublished document, 1995).
3. Wilkins, Thurman, *Cherokee* Tragedy, 2nd. Ed. (Norman: University of Oklahoma Press, 1986).
4. Satz, Ronald N. *American Indian Policy in the Jacksonian Era* (Lincoln: University of Nebraska, 1975).
5. Ehle, John *TRAIL of TEARS the Rise and fall of the Cherokee Nation* (Anchor Books/Doubleday, New York, 1988).
6. Shackford, James A. and Folmsbee, Stanley J. *The Life of David Crockett of the State of Tennessee* A Facsimile Edition (Knoxville: University of Tennessee Press, 1973).
7. King, Duane H. *The Cherokee Indian Nation: A Troubled History* (Knoxville: University of Tennessee Press, 1979).
8. Johnson, Charles Blake, *The Last Beloved Woman* (Townsend: American Trail Books, 1994).
9. Brewer, Alberta and Carson *Valley So Wild a Folk History* (Knoxville: East Tennessee Historical Society, 1975).
10. Dykeman, Wilma, *The Tall Woman* (New York: Holt, Rinehart and Winston, 1962).
11. Montgomery, Michael B. and Hall, Joseph S. *Dictionary of Smoky Mountain English* (Knoxville: University of Tennessee Press, 2004).
12. Gedney, Matt Living *on the Unicoi Road: Helen's Pioneer Century and Tales from the Georgia Gold Rush* (Marietta: Little Star Press, 1996).
13. Ledford, Reba Rigsbee *Looking Back: The Memories of Reba Ledford Rigsbee* (Unpublished document, March, 1998).
14. http//www.rosecity.net/tears/trail/chief.html
15. http//www.ngeorgia.com/history/nghisttt.html
16. http//www.clanmatheson.org.chief.html
17. http//www.electricscotland.com/webclans/m/matheso2.html
18. *Clay County Heritage* – North Carolina, Vol. 1, p. 91, 1994.
19. Padgett, J. Guy, Chairman *Clay County 1861-1961* (Historical Committee, Clay County, North Carolina, 1961).
20. Browder, Nathaniel C. *The Cherokee Indians and Those who came after* (University of Tennessee Library Archives, Library of Congress 74-25553, Hayesville, NC, 1974).

21. Murray, Glenda Prater *Genealogy Notes* (Unpublished document, 2006).

22. McAllister, Anne Williams *Through Four Generations: Heinrich Weidner 1717-1792 Catharina Mull Weidner 1733-1804* (Library of Congress Catalogue Card Number: 92-64119, Hickory, North Carolina, 1992).

23. Matheson, Jack Douglas *A Memorial to a Grand Old Mountain* (The "Clay County Progress News," February 27, 2006).

24. Brands, H. W. *Andrew Jackson His Life and Times* (New York: Doubleday Random House, Inc., 2005).

25. Jahoda, Gloria *The Story of the American Indian Removal 1813-1855* (New York: Holt Rhinhart and Winston, 1975).

26. Mull, B. Rondal and Mabel M. *Mull Families of North Carolina History and Genealogy* (Genealogy Publishing Service, Franklin, North Carolina, 1997).

27. http//www.hartshorn.us

28. Crawford, Rebecca *The First Matheson Family in Western North Carolina* (Calvin McClung Historical Collection, East Tennessee Historical Center, 2006).

29. White, Alice D. Ed. *The Heritage of Cherokee County North Carolina* (Cherokee County Historical Museum Council, Volume I, 1987).

30. Padgett, Guy *A History of Clay County North Carolina* (McClung Collection, Lawson McGhee Library, Knoxville, Tennessee, 1987).

31. http//www.ancestry.com – 1860 United States Federal Census, 2005.

32. Sharpe, Bill *A New Geography of North Carolina* (Volume IV, Clay County, Sharpe Publishing Company, Inc., 1965).

33. http//www.cviog.uga.edu/Projects/gainfo/page.php?tdgh=1

34. www.cviog.uga.edu/Projects/gainfo/histcountyhmaps/ga1822map.htm

35. http//www.cviog.uga.edu/Projects/gainfo/sequoyah.htm

36. http//www.cviog.edu/Projects/gainfo/watie.htm

37. http//www.cviog.uga.edu/Projects/gainfo/cheroke2.htm

Photo 26. My Witch Hazel

Witch Hazel still grows wild in Matheson Cove and is widely known for its medicinal value. The properties of the leaves and bark are similar, and are used in astringents, tonics, and sedatives. Witch Hazel is valuable as a pain-killer and for treatment of hemorrhages, dysentery and other ailments. It has long been used by North American Indians as poultices for painful swellings and tumors and for making curative teas. ***But, I grow it in my yard for its beauty!***

About the Author and Illustrator

Eva Nell Mull Wike, Ph.D., was born September 9, 1938, in Clay County, North Carolina, as the seventh child of Joseph David Mull and Martha Jane Wimpey Mull. Today, she lives with her husband, James Seymour Wike, Sr., in Oak Ridge, Tennessee. Her son, James Seymour Wike, Jr., M.D., and his wife, Catherine Anne Lange Wike, live nearby with their three sons.

James Seymour Wike, Sr., was born April 19, 1930, as the first child in Homer Howard Wike, Sr. and Jessie Marie Snelson Wike's family of seven boys. While growing up on a large farm along the Tuckaseegee River, in East Le Porte, NC, Jim was able to learn through exploring his world. His interest in art and natural talent in drawing were obvious at an early age. In school his teachers were quick to call on him to 'draw' murals for school exhibits. But his enthusiasm for the chemistry won out over his love of the art. Today he enjoys designing and creating works in stain glass. His latest studies in art were at the Scottsdale School of Art in Arizona. Presently, sharing his artistic talents with his grandsons has become his passion in the art.